THE BEST IN

RESTAURANT

CORPORATE IDENTITY

THE BEST IN

RESTAURANT
CORPORATE IDENTITY

CONSULTANT EDITOR
STAFFORD CLIFF

ROTOVISION

A QUARTO BOOK

Published by ROTOVISION SA
Route Suisse 9
CH-1295 Mies
Switzerland

Distributed to the trade in the
United States & Canada by
Watson-Guptill Publications
1515 Broadway
New York, NY 10036

ISBN 0–8230–6138–8

This book was designed and produced by
Quarto Publishing plc
6 Blundell Street
London N7 9BH

Creative Director: Richard Dewing
Designer: Wayne Blades
Editor: Viv Croot

Typeset in Great Britain by
Central Southern Typesetters, Eastbourne
Manufactured in Hong Kong by Regent Publishing Services Limited
Printed in Hong Kong by Leefung-Asco Printers Ltd

This book is dedicated to Dee Nolan and Angela
Mason at *Metropolitan Home Magazine (UK)*. It is
thanks to them I've eaten and photographed in
some of the world's best restaurants. I would also
like to acknowledge the help of Ann Berne, David
Brittain, Virginia Christensen, Andrew Cliff,
Ken Kirkwood, Gordon Larson, Brian Ma Siy,
Gayle Mason, Jonathan Scott.

Contents

Introduction

Why does a restaurant need a corporate identity? Surely nobody goes out to eat somewhere because of its menu design or the style of its lettering? But how do we know what the food is like if we have never been there before?

There was a time when the best restaurants simply had a blackboard on one wall on which the chef wrote the day's special. Sometimes, there was a single handwritten or typed sheet of paper that got passed around from one table to the next. Sometimes the food is literally on display: recently I ate in a wonderful old family restaurant in Athens, where the elderly matriarch described what the house specials were by bringing a plate of each from the kitchen; and in Japan, popular restaurants have replica plates of food proudly displayed in the window, so even if you can't read the menu, or don't speak the language, you can choose what you want to eat.

But now something has happened — three things in fact. Firstly, the growth of the leisure industry and the pattern of leisure time itself. Eating out has become a huge growth industry; very few people *need* to go to restaurants; they go partly for sustenance, partly for entertainment — a chance to meet friends, enjoy the evening over a meal without having to cook or wash up.

Many more people eat out than used to and fast food makes up 6 percent of the food market of the UK. There is now a wider choice of restaurants than there has ever been before. In the UK, an average of ten new restaurants are opening (and inevitably closing) every week and the same is true in most major cities of the world.

Secondly, food has changed. No longer is it just a choice of English, French, Italian, Chinese or Indian. Influential chefs such as Michel Guérard, Wolfgang Puck, Alice Waters, Fredy Girardet, Raymond Blanc, Albert Roux, Anton Mosimann and their colleagues have changed the way we eat and transformed the experience of eating out — and on the way become as famous as film stars. Even airlines have employed famous name chefs to consult on their food. Menus can now feature any number of cross cultural ingredients and influences. Restaurant critics have been quick to pick up on these developments and cookery books and magazines have helped introduce it to a much wider audience.

Thirdly, design has changed. Now every design course and every design student's portfolio includes the design of a restaurant identity. In the late 1980s there was an enormous growth of small design studios; their overheads were lower, so they could afford to work on smaller projects for smaller fees. And since in many cases this younger generation was precisely the target market that the new trendy restaurants were trying to hit, it was logical that they should be asked to design the graphics that would attract people like themselves.

The corporate identity is now well established as an important element in the personality of a company: it tells the people who work there (or who want to work there) exactly what the company does, what it believes in, whether it is modern or traditional, international or regional, large or small; it tells its customers (actual and potential) about the quality of its products,

its service and its prices. Designers were quick to point out that a corporate identity is just as applicable to a restaurant as to, say, a computer company or a shop, and restaurateurs were quick to adopt the idea, especially when it came to launching new projects. Nobody wants to eat in a new restaurant if it's empty and prior to opening, a new restaurant — like a new musical — needs as much hype, PR and image-building as it can get. The design of an opening invitation for a restaurant can be the deciding factor in whether the guests come or not, just as much as a theatre poster can be in attracting an audience.

So what are the elements in a restaurant's corporate identity? Very few restaurants can afford to advertise unless they are in a hotel or part of a large chain. The fascia is the obvious place to put the name, but in fact the choice of building and location can say much more about the patron. Many restaurants hire architects to design their interior space if not the building itself — and if it is a foreign architect, even better. The Japanese are particularly keen on flying Europeans or Americans over to work on their restaurants. Phillippe Starck, Nigel Coates and Joseph Lembo have all designed restaurants in Japan. Sometimes the

architect, or their team, will even design the logo too. If not, by the time the graphic designer has been commissioned, the style of the food and the style of the building, even the interior space might well have been decided.

And of course the name is a key element. Often it is the name of the chef or the owner; sometimes it refers to the style of cuisine and sometimes the locale. It may even be a legacy: when Franck Cerutti, a young chef in Nice, took over an existing restaurant just off the Promenade des Anglaises, the large illuminated letters on the façade bore the name 'Don Camillo', given by the previous owner. Working to a tight budget, Cerutti decided to leave the name up and spend his money on the interior and commissioned wonderful graphics from his friend Wilhelm Schlote for the menus and business cards. Consequently, the exterior of the restaurant bears no relationship to the graphic identity.

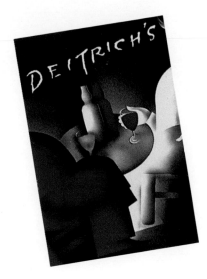

Menus were once the prime purveyor of the graphic content. They have a large cover surface (sometimes too large for the small menu and even smaller tables) which offers an ideal place for the designer to have some fun. Sometimes the menu is just a single sheet overprinted each day or each time the food changes. Sometimes it is a cover inside which reposes an elaborate document of many pages; this sort of menu may be printed, embossed, bound, laminated or in some cases, edged in brass — and never, ever changes.

Nowadays, with PR agents often commissioned to handle the promotion of a restaurant, dozens of other elements have been invented or adopted to purvey the personality of a place. Matchboxes are not so new, but you can now pick up business cards, souvenir postcards, T-shirts, sweat shirts, baseball caps, pens, pencils, posters, preserves, paper hats, masks, balloons, wine labels, doggie bags, car stickers, napkins, recipe books and of course the ubiquitous ashtray. Sometimes these are so desirable (and so expensive) that the staff are instructed to add the price to the bill if they notice that one is missing. The ashtrays in London's Bibendum restaurant feature a three dimensional M. Bibendum sitting on one side and are a status symbol in themselves.

So now it's a complete free for all, an anarchy that produces some very interesting and exciting results. There are no set rules for design or food. Painters design signage, architects design logos and interiors, chefs even do their own graphics, PR firms determine the client profile. Dozens of food combinations put together influences from every part of the world; traditional, even old-fashioned food co-exists with modern, ethnic and regional combinations; you can choose between famous chefs and themed 'experiences', international fast food and suburban home cooking. And every graphic and interior designer worth their salt is creating ever more innovative and mouth-watering design.

In this book, I have included a very broad selection of design solutions drawn from around the world. This is not an elite selection of prize-winning work, but rather a source for ideas and inspiration and a record for future reference.

Cafés, Brasseries and Bar-Grills

Generally speaking, people are less likely to go to these places for food; it's more often the atmosphere, the interior, the music, the location or the crowd that is the attraction. Consequently, the design concept has to work harder and be more imaginative if it is to make a memorable impression and appeal to the target customer.

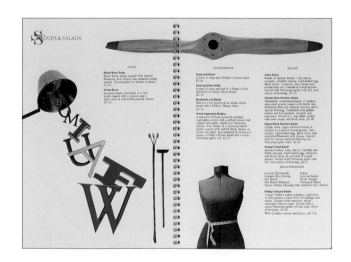

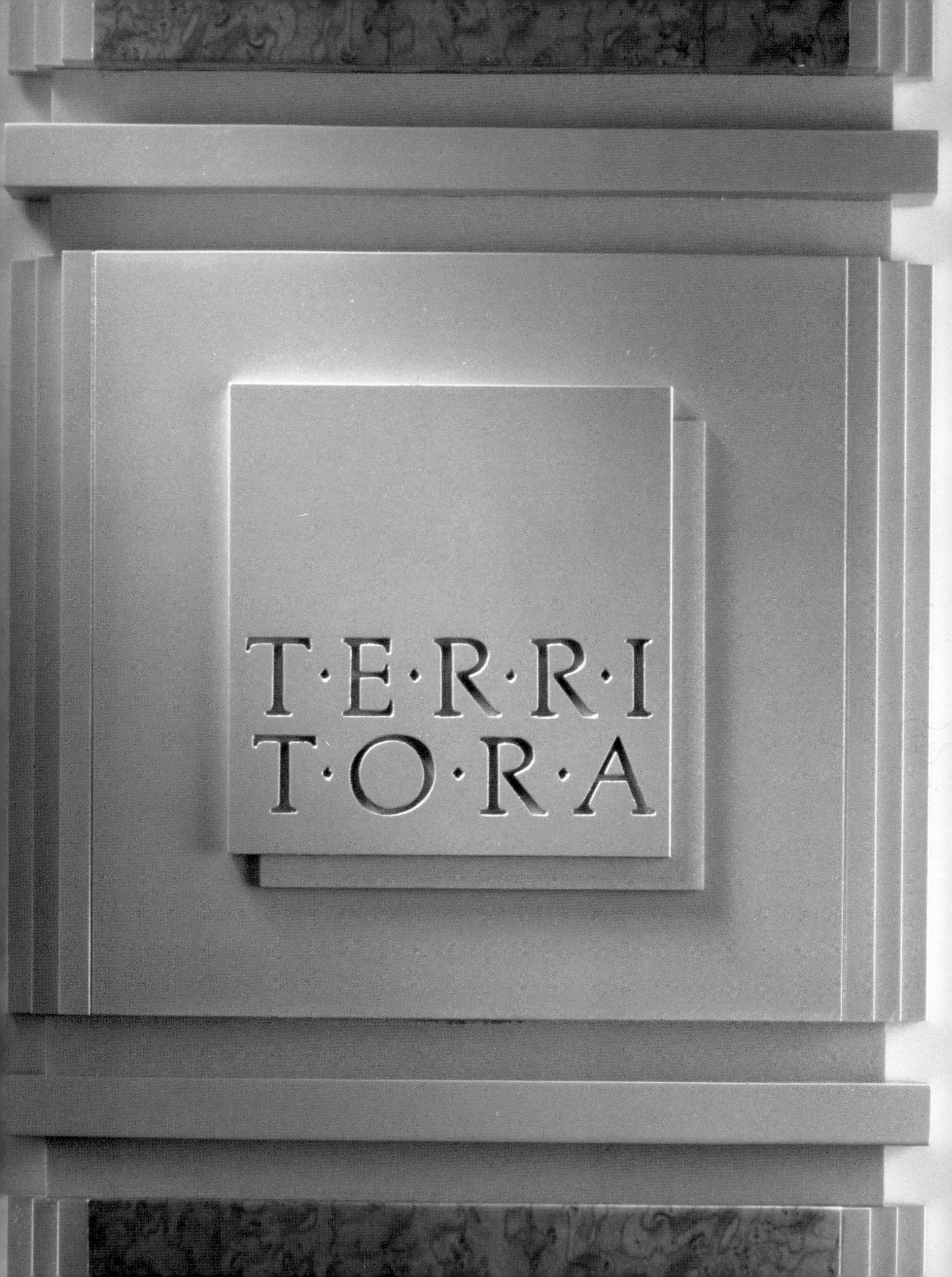
T·E·R·R·I
T·O·R·A

Territora

ADDRESS: Orly Airport West, Paris, France

STYLE OF FOOD: Snacks, sandwiches, patisserie

NO OF SEATS: None; stand-up venue

DESIGNER (Interior): Gérard Moratille/GBGM, Paris, France

DESIGNER (Graphics): S. D'Argent/GBGM, Paris, France

DATE OF COMPLETION: April 1991

GRAPHIC ELEMENTS: Logo, china

For an airport bar, this project mercifully avoids pretensiousness and complication and all the trappings of travel imagery.

TGI Friday's

ADDRESS: Nationwide UK and USA

CHEF: Various

STYLE OF FOOD: International

NO OF SEATS: Average 250

DESIGNER (Interior): TGI Friday's, New York City, New York, USA

DESIGNER (Graphics): TGI Friday's, New York City, New York, USA

DATE OF COMPLETION: 1965

GRAPHIC ELEMENTS: Menu, logo, napkins, plates, matchboxes

I like the way the menu successfully reflects the eclectic nature of the interior; if the objects had had captions it would have been even better.

TGI Friday's continued over page

TGI Friday's continued

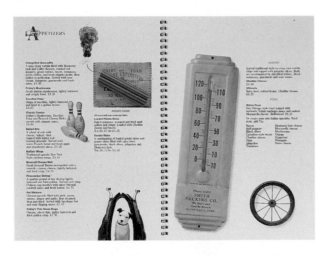

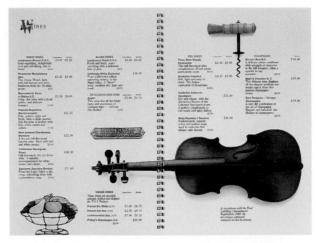

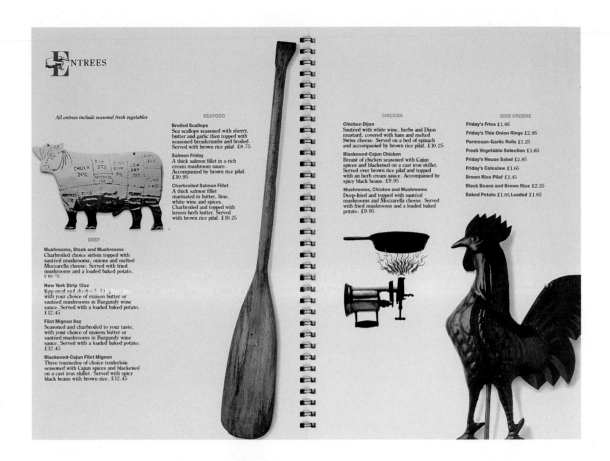

Entrees

All entrees include seasonal fresh vegetables

SEAFOOD

Broiled Scallops
Sea scallops seasoned with sherry, butter and garlic then topped with seasoned breadcrumbs and broiled. Served with brown rice pilaf. £8.75

Salmon Friday
A thick salmon fillet in a rich cream mushroom sauce. Accompanied by brown rice pilaf. £10.95

Charbroiled Salmon Fillet
A thick salmon fillet marinated in butter, lime, white wine and spices. Charbroiled and topped with lemon-herb butter. Served with brown rice pilaf. £10.25

BEEF

Mushrooms, Steak and Mushrooms
Charbroiled choice sirloin topped with sautéed mushrooms, onions and melted Mozzarella cheese. Served with fried mushrooms and a loaded baked potato. £10.75

New York Strip 12oz
Seasoned and charbroiled with your choice of maison butter or sautéed mushrooms in Burgundy wine sauce. Served with a loaded baked potato. £12.45

Filet Mignon 8oz
Seasoned and charbroiled to your taste, with your choice of maison butter or sautéed mushrooms in Burgundy wine sauce. Served with a loaded baked potato. £12.45

Blackened-Cajun Filet Mignon
Three tournedos of choice tenderloin seasoned with Cajun spices and blackened on a cast iron skillet. Served with spicy black beans with brown rice. £12.45

CHICKEN

Chicken Dijon
Sautéed with white wine, herbs and Dijon mustard, covered with ham and melted Swiss cheese. Served on a bed of spinach and accompanied by brown rice pilaf. £10.25

Blackened-Cajun Chicken
Breast of chicken seasoned with Cajun spices and blackened on a cast iron skillet. Served over brown rice pilaf and topped with an herb cream sauce. Accompanied by spicy black beans. £9.95

Mushrooms, Chicken and Mushrooms
Deep-fried and topped with sautéed mushrooms and Mozzarella cheese. Served with fried mushrooms and a loaded baked potato. £9.95

SIDE ORDERS

Friday's Fries £1.05
Friday's Thin Onion Rings £2.95
Parmesan-Garlic Rolls £1.25
Fresh Vegetable Selection £1.65
Friday's House Salad £2.85
Friday's Coleslaw £1.65
Brown Rice Pilaf £1.45
Black Beans and Brown Rice £2.25
Baked Potato £1.05, **Loaded** £1.65

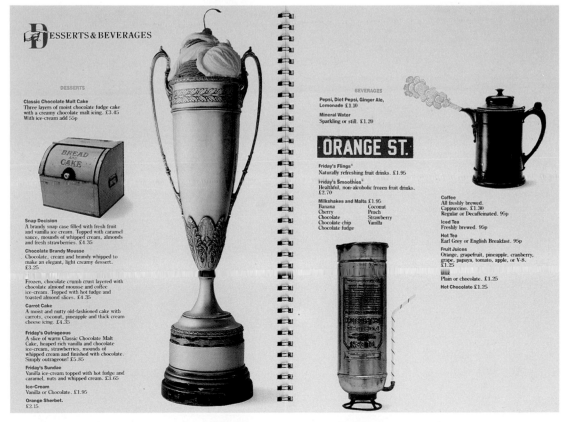

Desserts & Beverages

DESSERTS

Classic Chocolate Malt Cake
Three layers of moist chocolate fudge cake with a creamy chocolate malt icing. £3.45
With ice-cream add 55p

Snap Decision
A brandy snap case filled with fresh fruit and vanilla ice cream. Topped with caramel sauce, mounds of whipped cream, almonds and fresh strawberries. £4.35

Chocolate Brandy Mousse
Chocolate, cream and brandy whipped to make an elegant, light creamy dessert. £3.25

Frozen, chocolate crumb crust layered with chocolate almond mousse and coffee ice-cream. Topped with hot fudge and toasted almond slices. £4.35

Carrot Cake
A moist and nutty old-fashioned cake with carrots, coconut, pineapple and thick cream cheese icing. £4.35

Friday's Outrageous
A slice of warm Classic Chocolate Malt Cake, heaped rich vanilla and chocolate ice-cream, strawberries, mounds of whipped cream and finished with chocolate. Simply outrageous! £5.85

Friday's Sundae
Vanilla ice-cream topped with hot fudge and caramel, nuts and whipped cream. £3.65

Ice-Cream
Vanilla or Chocolate. £1.95

Orange Sherbet.
£2.15

BEVERAGES

Pepsi, Diet Pepsi, Ginger Ale, Lemonade £1.10

Mineral Water
Sparkling or still. £1.20

Friday's Flings®
Naturally refreshing fruit drinks. £1.95

Friday's Smoothies®
Healthful, non-alcoholic frozen fruit drinks. £2.70

Milkshakes and Malts £1.95
Banana · Coconut
Cherry · Peach
Chocolate · Strawberry
Chocolate chip · Vanilla
Chocolate fudge

Coffee
All freshly brewed.
Cappuccino. £1.30
Regular or Decaffeinated. 95p

Iced Tea
Freshly brewed. 96p

Hot Tea
Earl Grey or English Breakfast. 95p

Fruit Juices
Orange, grapefruit, pineapple, cranberry, grape, papaya, tomato, apple, or V-8. £1.25

Plain or chocolate. £1.25

Hot Chocolate £1.25

17

LiVE bAiT

NO MONKEY BUSINESS! WE GIVE SERVICE

★ Starters ★

★ CHEF'S SOUP OF THE SEASON .... cup $2.95 / bowl $3.95

★ CUP OF PLANTATION GUMBO $3.45

★ bAit SHACK SPECIALS - SEE OUR bLACKbOARD. For today's selection of oysters + clams (priced accord.)

★ CAROLINA bbQ CHICKEN WINGS (marinated in Live bait's mildly spicy bbQ sauce) ... $3.95

★ CHEDDAR CHEESE AND JALAPEÑO HUSH PUPPIES $3.25

★ MARYLAND bACKFIN CRAbCAKE $5.95

★ CHILLED GULF SHRIMP COCKTAIL $5.95

★ GRILLED bARbEQUED SHRIMP SERVED ON A SKEWER WITH OUR FAMOUS CORN RELISH $6.95

★ CAJUN FRIED CALAMARI SERVED WITH A SPICY MARINARA $5.95

★ TOSSED SEASONAL GREENS WITH JULIENNE VEGETAbLES $3.50

★ CLASSIC COUNTRY COBB SALAD .... $4.95 / AS AN ENTREE $7.95

★ SALADS ★

★ CHAR GRILLED SHRIMP AND CHICKEN SALAD SERVED WITH bALSAMIC VINEGARETTE AND SEASONAL GREENS ... $7.95

★ KEY WEST CEVICHÉ WITH CILANTRO, AVOCADO, LIME, PEPPERS, AND RED ONIONS $5.95

★ GRILLED bREAST OF CHICKEN SERVED ON A bED OF SEASONAL GREENS WITH APPLES, PECANS, AND bLUE CHEESE WITH bALSAMIC VINEGARETTE ... $7.95

Try our DELICIOUS BAR-B-Q

WE AIM TO PLEASE

Check Our Specials Board

"Have a Coke"

Sea Food OUR SPECIALTY

Bottoms Up

Vegetables

no Pipes or cigars in Dining room PLEASE.

WE ACCEPT reservations for parties of 8 or more.

PICK-UP: Cuts service and delivery costs.

SEDAN: Over 20,000 now on the road.

for a Light Lunch

★ SANDWICHES ★ LiVE bAiT

★ LAYERS OF CHICKEN, MARINATED IN LEMON LIME AND GARLIC, CHARCOAL GRILLED AND SERVED ON A SESAME ROLL W/ HONEY MUSTARD DIJONAISE SAUCE $6.95

★ PULLED CAROLINA PORK bbQ ON A bUN $6.95

★ MARYLAND SHORE CRAB CAKE SANDWICH w/HOMEMADE TARTAR SAUCE ... $8.95

★ CHATTANOOGA CHEESE STEAK ... $7.95

★ TURKEY, AVOCADO, TOMATO AND bACON SERVED ON WHOLE WHEAT WITH JALAPEÑO MAYONAISE ... $7.95

★ CHICKEN FRIED CATFISH SANDWICH ... $6.50 (100% FARM RAISED CATFISH FILET)

★ DELUXE HAMbURGER PLATTER ... $5.75 CHEDDAR, AMERICAN, SWISS, AVOCADO, bACON OR FRIED ONIONS ... 75¢ EACH

ALL SANDWICHES ARE SERVED W/ LETTUCE, TOMATO AND RAW ONION AND A CHOICE OF FRENCH FRIES OR COLE SLAW.

★ ENTREES ★

★ AUNT bEA'S bOARDING HOUSE FRIED CHICKEN ... $7.95 (ALL WHITE MEAT ADD $1.25)

★ PLANTATION GUMBO - MADE WITH CAJUN SAUSAGE PORK SHRIMP + CHICKEN, SERVED W/ WHITE RICE ... $6.95

★ JAIL HOUSE CHILI SERVED W/ STEAMED RICE, CHEDDAR CHEESE, CHOPPED ONIONS AND SOUR CREAM ... $6.95

★ ROBERT E. LEE'S CHICKEN FRIED STEAK w/ CREAM GRAVY ... $10.25

★ FARM RAISED DELTA CATFISH FILET ... $9.95 w/ CRUNCHY CORNFLAKE bREADING + PECAN bUTTER or GRILLED w/ CRACKED bLACK PEPPER + LEMON

GOOD FOODS SERVED RIGHT

★ FIXINS (choose one) ★
FRESH VEGETABLE OF THE DAY, BLACK EYED PEAS, COLLARD GREENS, RED BEANS, COLE SLAW, FRENCH FRIES, MASHED POTATOES w/ GRAVY

(EXTRA SIDE ... $1.25)

LARGE PARTIES ARE SUBJECT TO 17.5% SERVICE CHARGE.

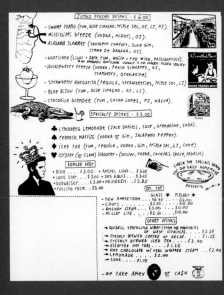

Jumbo Frozen Drinks - $6.00

● SWAMP THANG (rum, blue curacao, triple sec, OJ, LT, PJ)

● MISSISSIPPI breeze (vodka, midori, OJ)

● ALABAMA SLAMMER (southern comfort, sloe gin, creme de banana, OJ)

● HURRICANE (light + dark rum, white + red wine, passionfruit) OUR ORIGINAL HURRICANE USUALLY IS OUR STRONG - PLEASE SPECIFY

● HUCKLEBERRY FREEZE (vodka, peach schnapps, OJ, cranberry, grenadine)

● STRAWBERRY MARGARITA (tequila, strawberries, triple sec, LT)

● BLUE bIJOU (rum, blue curacao, OJ, LT)

● CROCODILE bLENDEE (rum, cocoa lopez, PJ, kalua)

Specialty Drinks - $5.00

♣ LYNCHbERG LEMONADE (JACK DANIELS, SOUR, GRENADINE, SODA)

♠ REDNECK MARTINI (VODKA or GIN, JALAPEÑO PEPPER)

♦ ICED TEA (RUM, TEQUILA, VODKA, GIN, TRIPLE SEC, LT, COKE)

♥ OYSTER (or CLAM) SHOOTER (OYSTER, VODKA, COCKTAIL SAUCE, TABASCO)

bOTTLED bEER
• DIXIE ... $3.00 • AMSTEL LIGHT ... $3.25
• LONE STAR ... $3.00 • DOS EQUIS ... $3.25
• bUDWEISER ... $3.00 • HEINEKEN ... $3.25
• ROLLING ROCK ... $3.00

CHECK THE SPECIALS BOARD FOR OUR DAILY HOMEMADE Desserts

ON TAP | GLASS | PITCHER
• NEW AMSTERDAM | $2.75 | $11.00
• COORS | $2.50 | $10.00
• ANCHOR STEAM | $3.00 | $11.00
• MILLER LITE | $2.50 | $10.00

OTHER DRINKS
• QUIbELL SPARKLING WATER (FROM THE MOUNTAINS OF WEST VIRGINIA) ... $2.25
• FRESHLY bREWED COFFEE OR DECAF ... $1.25
• FRESHLY bREWED ICED TEA ... $2.00
• ASSORTED HOT TEAS ... $1.25
• HOT CHOCOLATE w/ REAL WHIPPED CREAM ... $2.00
• LEMONADE ... $2.00
• SODA ... $1.75

- WE TAKE AMEX or CASH

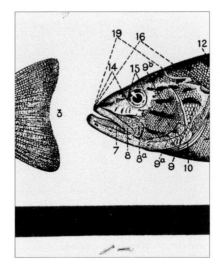

CLOSE COVER

Live Bait

ADDRESS: New York City, New York, USA

CHEF: David Corsin

STYLE OF FOOD: Southeast Regional

NO. OF SEATS: 90

DESIGNER (Interior): Charles Milite, Carolyn Effer, Eric Petterson/Manhatten Design, New York City, New York, USA

DESIGNER (Graphics): Frank Oliskaye/Manhatten Design, New York City, New York, USA

DATE OF COMPLETION: September 1987

GRAPHIC ELEMENTS: Menus, stationery, matchbooks, posters, takeaway stickers

A very personal, almost non-designed solution, that says everything about the restaurant and its view of life.

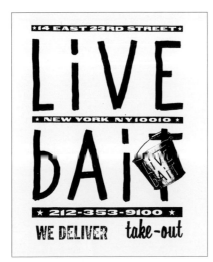

VORA
MAR

Restaurant

VORA
MAR

Bar Restaurant

Consolat de Mar, 90
Tel. 36 13 28
Cambrils Port

VORA MAR

VORA MAR

Tapas

Bar

VORA MAR

Bar Restaurant
Consolat de Mar, 90
Tel. 36 13 28
Cambrils Port

Voramar

ADDRESS: Tarragona, Spain

CHEF: Mª Carmen Rodriguez

STYLE OF FOOD: Snack Bar

NO. OF SEATS: 100

DESIGNER (Interior): Estevo Agullo and Mariano Pi/
Quod, Barcelona, Spain

DESIGNER (Graphics): Josep Trias Mª Quod,
Barcelona, Spain

DATE OF COMPLETION: 1989

GRAPHIC ELEMENTS: Matchboxes, menu

This is what we used to call 'Swiss Typography'
when I was at school. Somehow surprising to find
such a solution coming out of Spain; I find its
freshness shocking, like a splash of cold water in
the face.

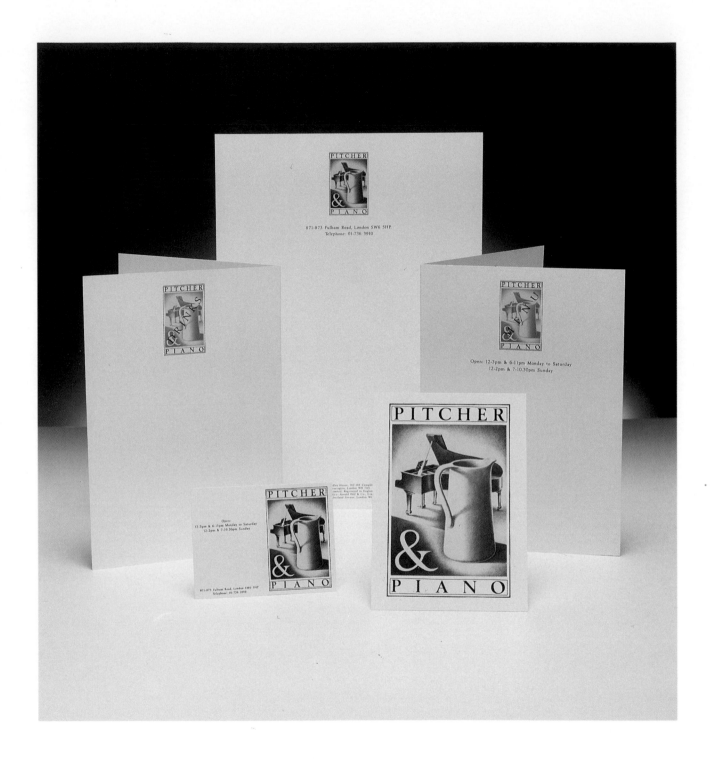

Pitcher & Piano

ADDRESS: Small chain, London, England

CHEF: Various

STYLE OF FOOD: Eclectic

NO OF SEATS: 100

DESIGNER (Graphics): Jim Allen, The Team, London, England

DATE OF COMPLETION: 1988

GRAPHIC ELEMENTS: External signage, menus, napkins, matchbooks, promotional literature

Combining the relaxed qualities of a piano bar with those of a pub was how the designer described the project. The illustration (by Alastair Taylor) refers to the hanging signs traditional to British pubs, but in black and white it suggests a more sophisticated clientele.

Brasserie Rocque

ADDRESS: London, England

CHEF: Nick Guana

STYLE OF FOOD: French

NO. OF SEATS: 126

DESIGNER (Interior): Alistair Fleming, Design House, London, England

DESIGNER (Graphics): Chris Lower, Design House, London, England

DATE OF COMPLETION: 1988

GRAPHIC ELEMENTS: Wine labels, menus, wine lists, matchboxes, napkin rings, business cards, signs

This is much more than a simple restaurant identity; it's a beautifully executed series of elements where every ingredient – typography, paper, illustrations and colours – works in harmony. A very 'modern' solution crafted from traditional elements.

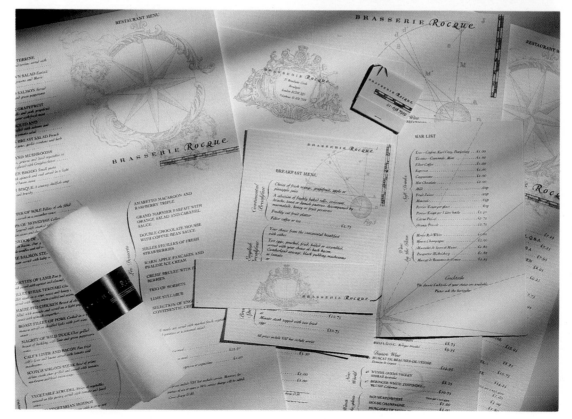

Duwamp's Café & Seattle Brewing Company

ADDRESS: Seattle, Washington, USA

STYLE OF FOOD: Café

NO. OF SEATS: 100

DESIGNER (Interior): Girvin Design, Seattle, Washington, USA

DESIGNER (Graphics): Tim Girvin, Stephen Pannone Girvin Design, Seattle, Washington, USA

DATE OF COMPLETION: 1990

GRAPHIC ELEMENTS: Menu

Cafe Le Moko

ADDRESS: Chicago, Illinois, USA

CHEF: Errol McIntire

STYLE OF FOOD: Café-style, brunch

NO. OF SEATS: 150

DESIGNER (Graphics): Wayne Kosterman,
John Anderson/Identity Center, Schaumburg,
Illinois, USA

DATE OF COMPLETION: January 1991

GRAPHIC ELEMENTS: Menu

Mesa Grill

ADDRESS: New York City, New York, USA

CHEF: Bobby Flay

STYLE OF FOOD: American southwestern

NO. OF SEATS: 130

DESIGNER (Interior): James Biber Architect

DESIGNER (Graphics): Alexander Isley Design, New York City, New York, USA

DATE OF COMPLETION: January 1991

GRAPHIC ELEMENTS: Menus, matchbook, letterhead, cards

Very confident use of strong typography and abstract textures .

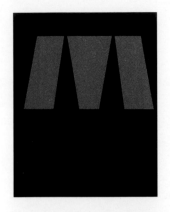

GRILL
102 Fifth Ave.
NY, NY 10011
212-807-7400

Houlihans

ADDRESS: Nationwide chain, USA

STYLE OF FOOD: Casual dining; cocktails

NO. OF SEATS: Varies

DESIGNER (Graphics): Chuck Pollard, Gilbert/
Robinson Inc, Kansas City Missouri, USA;
photography: Bob Frame

DATE OF COMPLETION: August 1990

GRAPHIC ELEMENTS: Menu

A nice fresh 'original' solution combining strong
fashion photography with magazine style
typography. No doubt at all who this bar is
targeted at.

OPTIONS: It's what living in America… and more and more of the world…is all about. OPTIONS means the freedom to create your own worktime, playtime, lifetime. And when it comes to refreshment, it means drinking with your attitude as much in mind as your thirst. Whether your personal timing calls for a quick beer, a light pick-me-up, a non-alcoholic thirst quencher, or a good old-fashioned Old Fashioned, Houlihan's serves up your OPTIONS—hot or cold, but always bold. The choice is yours.

HOULIHAN'S

Photography by BOB FRAME Produced by Houlie 100 © Gilbert/Robinson, Inc. 1990

OPTION CLASSICS

TRADITION—NOT NECESSARILY WHAT EVERYONE HAS DONE THROUGH HISTORY, BUT WHAT YOU DO TODAY WITH A SENSE OF HISTORY.

BLUE WHALE
Blue Curaçao, Midori, Sprite & a whale of course!

CHEAP SUNGLASSES
Vodka, Sprite, cranberry juice & shades.

PEPPER MARY
Made hot with peppered vodka and a seasoned rim.

LAST DATE
Vodka, cranberry juice and pear soda.

CACTUS BOWL
Captain Morgan, Bacardi 151 and Amaretto with pineapple & lime juice. Limit two.

GRAND GOLD MARGARITA
Cuervo Gold, Grand Marnier & a Cuervo shooter.

BIG JUAN MARGARITA
Texas-sized, with a warm like no other. Limit two.

KALIBER
If you love the taste of beer, but not the alcohol.

IRC ROOT BEER
Cold and refreshing, the rich old-time favorite.

OPTION SPRING WATER

TWO PARTS HYDROGEN TO ONE PART OXYGEN, YES. BUT WHY NOT MORE? WE INVITE YOU TO REPLACE YOUR BODY'S ESSENTIAL FLUID WITH SPARKLE.

CHAPELLE
Natural sparkling spring water in individual or table bottles.

CHAPELLE PEACH
Sparkling spring water with peach juice in individual bottles.

CHAPELLE PEAR
Natural pear flavored sparkling spring water in individual bottles.

CHAPELLE RASPBERRY
Natural raspberry flavored sparkling spring water in individual bottles.

EVIAN
Imported natural spring water in individual or table bottles.

OPTION COOL & CREAMY

WHEN THE GOING GETS TOUGH, THE TOUGH CHILL OUT. TRY OUR FROZEN ESCAPES…SOME WITH A LITTLE ALCOHOL, SOME WITH MORE, SOME YOU COULD SERVE A 10-YEAR-OLD…OR THE 10-YEAR-OLD IN YOU.

BERRYETTO
A creamy blend of Amaretto and strawberries.

COOKIE CRUSHER
Creme de Menthe, Creme de Cacao, and Oreo Cookies blended.

RUM BERRY ORANGE
Rum, orange juice, strawberries.

FIRST DATE
Amaretto, orange juice and Triple Sec.

MOCHACCINO
Jameson premium whiskey and coffee blended, creamy and lighter on the alcohol.

CHOCOLATE CHERRY
A chocolaty blend of Amaretto and cherry, light on the alcohol.

CHOCOLATE PEANUT
A non-alcoholic creamy mix of peanut butter and chocolate.

BERRY COLADA
A virgin mix of pineapple, Coco Lopez, and strawberries.

MINT COOKIE
Peppermint & Oreo Cookies in a non-alcoholic shake.

OPTION SALSA

WHEN THE SUN IS HOT OR THE NIGHT IS DARK, PASSIONATE RHYTHMS DEMAND COOLING ELIXIRS

BAHAMA MAMA
Myers's and Bacardi 151 Rum with Cream of Coconut & fruit juices.

BERMUDA TRIANGLE
Bacardi Light, Gold Reserve and 151 Rum with exotic fruit juices.

PINA COLADA
Coconut, pineapple juice and Bacardi Rum, original tropical refresher.

STRAWBERRY DAIQUIRI
Rum, strawberries, ice and enjoyment.

PEACH PUNCH
Peach Schnapps, Bacardi Light Rum, oj and Cream of Coconut.

CROCODILE COOLER
Lemon Vodka, Midori, sweet & sour and Sprite.

WILD BIRD
A light alcohol beverage with Peach Schnapps and exotic fruit juices.

BIRD TEASER
A non-alcoholic combination of cranberry, pineapple, papaya & apple juices with Sprite.

OPTION CAPPUCCINO

MAY WE CORDIALLY SUGGEST ONE OF OUR HEARTWARMING CORDIALS TO CAP YOUR CAPP? OR, WOULD YOU PREFER TO SIP INTO SOMETHING COMFORTABLE BELOW?

CAPPUCCINO HOULIHAN
Our own special blend with six liqueurs.

CAPPUCCINO CANCUN
With Sambuca, Baileys Irish Cream & Kahlua.

CAPPUCCINO NUT
With Frangelico and Baileys Irish Cream.

CAPPUCCINO MOCHA MINT
Peppermint Schnapps and white Creme de Cacao.

HOP SCOTCH
Hot cocoa with Butterscotch Schnapps and whipped cream—a lighter alcohol choice.

IRISH COFFEE
The Buena Vista® recipe with Jameson premium whiskey.

Your safety is important to us.
Please do not mix drinking and driving.
We would be happy to arrange transportation for you.

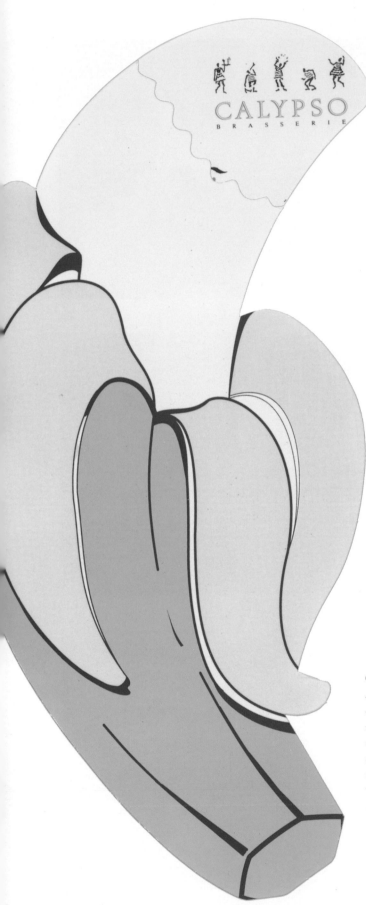

Calypso

ADDRESS: Glenelg, South Australia, Australia

CHEF: Ray Mauger

STYLE OF FOOD: Caribbean influenced

NO. OF SEATS: 140

DESIGNER (Interior): Terry Feltus Architect

DESIGNER (Graphics): Gayle Mason Design, Wayville, South Australia, Australia

DATE OF COMPLETION: October 1990

GRAPHIC ELEMENTS: Menus and placemats

Each 'shape' contains a different part of the menu: the apple for starters and main courses, the strawberry for puddings and coffee and so on.

CALYPSO

Starters

"From the ships that sailed the trade winds"

SOUP OF THE DAY

MARINATED OCTOPUS
Traditional as Calypso music — marinated Octopus served on flat bread with a garlic and yoghurt dressing.
$4.50

OYSTERS NATURAL (Serve of 10)
Ours are always the best — served in the half shell (freshly opened).
$7.50

GRILLED CHICKEN & MANGO
What a combination — diced, grilled chicken served on a mound of greens and delicious mango, topped with peppered vinaigrette dressing.
$10.90

AVOCADO & SHRIMP SALAD
Put shrimps, avocado slices, crisp bacon, Bermuda onions and toss them all with spinach greens and house dressing and you then know why the West Indians are so happy.
$7.90

BEEF SATAY
The finest we can make is yours for the asking — with a little spicy peanut sauce this will test your taste buds.
$6.90

Island Collection

FISH 'N' CHIPS
A tradition in any land — fresh fillets of fish in crispy beer batter with fries & tartare sauce.
$12.50

VIV RICHARDS SPECIAL
A fresh fillet of fish — grilled and topped with a delicate sauce of coconut, chilli & lime —
'a cricketer's dream'.
$11.50

PORK RIBS
The perfection of summer nights in the West Indies is close to this dish - prime ribs of pork cooked in our own special way, topped with a delicious spicy sauce — finger licking good!
$9.90

CALYPSO SHASLICKS
Nothing fancy - just prime beef marinated to perfection and then lightly charred on a skewer.
$10.90

ZUCCHINI TARTLET
Plump zucchini lightly spiced with pepper, baked in puff pastry with a tropical salad of avocado and over ripe tomato vinaigrette.

BREAD
Like mother used to make.
Mini loaf of grainy house bread.

CALYPSO FRIES (per serve) $1.50

SIDE SERVE OF MUSHROOMS (per serve) $3.90

The Calypso Burger!

"A burger like no other!"

First we take 1/3 pound of the finest hand chopped steak, cook it to perfection, then lay it on our chef's special roll and serve it with your choice of:

Crisp bacon, pineapple, fried egg & mango relish $8.50
OR Spicy tomato & chilli topping $9.50
OR Sautéed mushrooms & natural melted cheese $8.90

So here you have it! The best burger you have ever had.

Fast Food and Family
Restaurants There's potentially more fun to

be had designing graphics for this type of venue but it is

also sometimes harder to produce solutions that have

both family appeal and design integrity. Even then, it's

often only the cover of the menu that looks good; the

typography and the inside pages remain conservative

and uninspired.

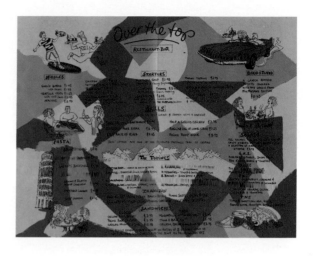

Burger King

ADDRESS: International chain, Burger King Headquarters, Miami, Florida, USA

CHEF: Various

STYLE OF FOOD: Fast food

NO. OF SEATS: 85 (average)

DESIGNER (Graphics): Donald Geisz, Linda Sheintop, Butch Quick, Bruce Handler, Anne Pedula/King Casey, New Canaan, Connecticut, USA

DATE OF COMPLETION: September 1990

GRAPHIC ELEMENTS: Menuboard, packaging, merchandising posters

BK Doubles

BK Doubles

BK Doubles

OCEAN CATCH
FISH FILET
ON AN OAT BRAN BUN

FLAME-BROILED
BK Broiler
CHICKEN SANDWICH

FLAME-BROILED
W
WHOPPER®

BURGER
KING

The Burger that ate LA

ADDRESS: Los Angeles, California, USA

STYLE OF FOOD: Burger and Family

NO. OF SEATS: 86

DESIGNER (Interior): Solberg & Lowe Architects

DESIGNER (Graphics): Gerry Rosentsweig/The Graphic Studio, Hollywood, Los Angeles, California, USA

DATE OF COMPLETION: April 1989

GRAPHIC ELEMENTS: Menu, T-shirt

This is a rare example of a restaurant where the building resembles the logo, rather than the reverse; and the burgers are delicious.

EZ's

ADDRESS: San Antonio, Texas, USA

STYLE OF FOOD: Pizzas, burgers, salads, shakes

NO. OF SEATS: 175

DESIGNER (Interior): Alamo Architects, Texas, USA

DESIGNER (Graphics): The Bradford Lawton Design
Group, San Antonio, Texas, USA

DATE OF COMPLETION: December 1989

GRAPHIC ELEMENTS: Matchboxes, menu, plates,
napkins

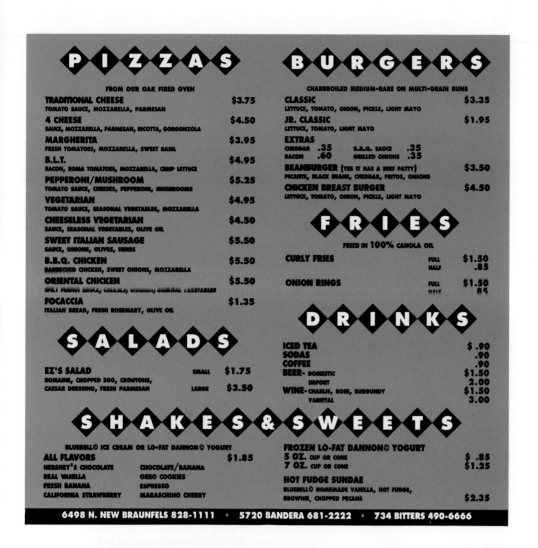

PIZZAS

FROM OUR OAK FIRED OVEN

TRADITIONAL CHEESE	$3.75
TOMATO SAUCE, MOZZARELLA, PARMESAN	
4 CHEESE	$4.50
SAUCE, MOZZARELLA, PARMESAN, RICOTTA, GORGONZOLA	
MARGHERITA	$3.95
FRESH TOMATOES, MOZZARELLA, SWEET BASIL	
B.L.T.	$4.95
BACON, ROMA TOMATOES, MOZZARELLA, CRISP LETTUCE	
PEPPERONI/MUSHROOM	$5.25
TOMATO SAUCE, CHEESES, PEPPERONI, MUSHROOMS	
VEGETARIAN	$4.95
TOMATO SAUCE, SEASONAL VEGETABLES, MOZZARELLA	
CHEESELESS VEGETARIAN	$4.50
SAUCE, SEASONAL VEGETABLES, OLIVE OIL	
SWEET ITALIAN SAUSAGE	$5.50
SAUCE, ONIONS, OLIVES, HERBS	
B.B.Q. CHICKEN	$5.50
BARBECUED CHICKEN, SWEET ONIONS, MOZZARELLA	
ORIENTAL CHICKEN	$5.50
SPICY PEANUT SAUCE, CHILLIES, CRUNCHY ORIENTAL VEGETABLES	
FOCACCIA	$1.35
ITALIAN BREAD, FRESH ROSEMARY, OLIVE OIL	

SALADS

EZ'S SALAD	SMALL	$1.75
ROMAINE, CHOPPED EGG, CROUTONS,		
CAESAR DRESSING, FRESH PARMESAN	LARGE	$3.50

BURGERS

CHARBROILED MEDIUM-RARE ON MULTI-GRAIN BUNS

CLASSIC	$3.35
LETTUCE, TOMATO, ONION, PICKLE, LIGHT MAYO	
JR. CLASSIC	$1.95
LETTUCE, TOMATO, LIGHT MAYO	
EXTRAS	
CHEDDAR .35 B.B.Q. SAUCE .35	
BACON .60 GRILLED ONIONS .35	
BEANBURGER (YES IT HAS A BEEF PATTY)	$3.50
PICANTE, BLACK BEANS, CHEDDAR, FRITOS, ONIONS	
CHICKEN BREAST BURGER	$4.50
LETTUCE, TOMATO, ONION, PICKLE, LIGHT MAYO	

FRIES

FRIED IN 100% CANOLA OIL

CURLY FRIES	FULL	$1.50
	HALF	.85
ONION RINGS	FULL	$1.50
	HALF	.85

DRINKS

ICED TEA	$.90
SODAS	.90
COFFEE	.90
BEER- DOMESTIC	$1.50
IMPORT	2.00
WINE-CHABLIS, ROSE, BURGUNDY	$1.50
VARIETAL	3.00

SHAKES & SWEETS

BLUEBELL© ICE CREAM OR LO-FAT DANNON© YOGURT

ALL FLAVORS	$1.85

HERSHEY'S CHOCOLATE	CHOCOLATE/BANANA
REAL VANILLA	OREO COOKIES
FRESH BANANA	ESPRESSO
CALIFORNIA STRAWBERRY	MARASCHINO CHERRY

FROZEN LO-FAT DANNON© YOGURT	
5 OZ. CUP OR CONE	$.85
7 OZ. CUP OR CONE	$1.25
HOT FUDGE SUNDAE	
BLUEBELL© HOMEMADE VANILLA, HOT FUDGE,	
BROWNIE, CHOPPED PECANS	$2.35

6498 N. NEW BRAUNFELS 828-1111 • 5720 BANDERA 681-2222 • 734 BITTERS 490-6666

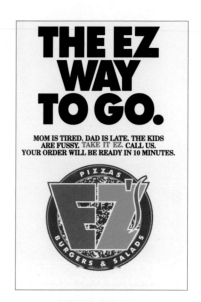

THE EZ WAY TO GO.

MOM IS TIRED. DAD IS LATE. THE KIDS ARE FUSSY. TAKE IT EZ. CALL US. YOUR ORDER WILL BE READY IN 10 MINUTES.

BETWEEN A HARD ROCK & THIS PLACE.

EVER GET TIRED OF SEEING THEIR SHIRTS EVERYWHERE? EZ'S T-SHIRTS ARE DEFINITELY COOLER, DUDE.

Open house begins on December 16th, 4 to 8 pm, at our newest EZ's, 5720 Bandera Rd. at Loop 410. You and a Guest are invited. Those attending will receive an EZ's Cap, complete with bill.

PSST... COME BY LATER

AFTER THE SHOW, CELEBRATE THE GAME OR JUST A NIGHTCAP BEFORE WE GO TO YOUR PLACE. EZ'S IS WAITING UP LATE FOR YOU. OPEN TIL 11 ON WEEKNIGHTS, 12 ON WEEKENDS.

Food Street

ADDRESS: London, England

CHEF: Various

STYLE OF FOOD: Street Chinese, Indian, Malaysian, Sushi, Japanese

NO. OF SEATS: 150

DESIGNER (Interior): Godsmark Gordon, London, England

DESIGNER (Graphics): Godsmark Gordon, London, England

DATE OF COMPLETION: May 1989

GRAPHIC ELEMENTS: Logos (for all concessions), menus, matchboxes, takeaway bags, napkins

The 'Food Court' in the heart of London's West End is transformed by graphics into a street in downtown Hong Kong.

Ed's Easy Diner

ADDRESS: London, England

STYLE OF FOOD: American-style burgers

NO. OF SEATS: 30

DESIGNER (Interior): Design House, London, England

DESIGNER (Graphics): Design House, London, England

DATE OF COMPLETION: July 1988

GRAPHIC ELEMENTS: Menus, stationery, clock, leaflets, neon signs

Even the striptease sign reflected in the glass of this 1950's style diner doesn't seem out of place with the brash, colourful neon façade. The expanse of glass and easy visual access into the interior is as important to the concept as the typography.

Compañia General de Sandwiches

ADDRESS: Chain of two restaurants, Barcelona, Spain

CHEF: Roberto Rolando

STYLE OF FOOD: Fast food and sandwiches

NO. OF SEATS: 40 and 90

DESIGNER (Interior): Carlos Rolando, CR Communication & Design Services SA, Barcelona, Spain

DESIGNER (Graphics): Carlos Rolando, CR Communication & Design Services SA, Barcelona, Spain

DATE OF COMPLETION: October 1980 and November 1983

GRAPHIC ELEMENTS: Logo, menu, calendars, takeaway bags, brochures, posters

Even the humble sandwich has a story to tell.

UNA BIOGRAFIA

BREVE HISTORIA DEL SANDWICH

Reproducido de "Cómo acabar de una vez por todas con la cultura". Woody Allen, 1986. Tusquets Editores

Sandwich, John Montagu, 4.º Conde de Nájar en Londres el 3 de noviembre de 1719 y muerte el 30 de abril de 1792 en el Balear (Inglés)

En serio

John Montagu Sandwich

1718 nace el Conde de Sandwich en una familia de aristócratas. El padre está encantado por haber sido nombrado jefe herrador de Su Majestad el Rey, posición de la que disfruta durante bastantes años hasta que descubre que no es más que un herrero y renuncia amargado. La madre es una simple *hausfrau* de extracción germánica cuyo sencillo menú consiste esencialmente en manteca de cerdo y avenate, aunque a veces demuestra cierta imaginación culinaria al confeccionar un postre de natas, huevos, vino y azúcar.

1725-1735 asiste a la escuela donde aprende a montar a caballo, y latín. En la escuela toma contacto por primera vez con los embutidos y muestra especial interés por los cortes muy finos de roast beef y de jamón. Para cuando se gradúa, esto se ha convertido ya en una obsesión y, aunque su tesis sobre "El análisis y los fenómenos concomitantes de la merienda de la tarde" llama la atención de los profesores, sus compañeros de estudio le consideran estrambótico.

1736 ingresa en la universidad de Cambridge, a instancias de sus padres, para seguir estudios de retórica y metafísica, pero muestra poco entusiasmo por los mismos. En constante rebelión contra todo lo académico, es acusado de robar pan y de llevar a cabo experimentos antinaturales con ese material. Las acusaciones de herejía determinan su expulsión.

1738 desheredado, se refugia en los países escandinavos donde, durante tres años, estudia intensivamente el queso. Fascinado por la gran variedad de sardinas que encuentra, anota en su cuaderno: "estoy convencido de que existe una realidad permanente, más allá de lo que aún ha podido lograr el hombre, en la yuxtaposición de los alimentos. Simplifica, simplifica".
A su regreso a Inglaterra conoce a Nell Smallbore, la hija de un verdulero, y contrae matrimonio. Ella le enseñará todo sobre la lectura.

Nell Smallbore

1741 residente en el campo con una modesta herencia, trabaja día y noche, apretando con frecuencia el cinturón para ahorrar y comprar comida. Su primera obra completa (una rebanada de pan, otra rebanada de pan encima de la primera y un trozo de pavo encima de las dos rebanadas) fracasa miserablemente. Desilusionado hasta la amargura, regresa a su estudio y vuelve a empezarlo todo de nuevo.

1745 después de cuatro años de frenética labor, está convencido de haber alcanzado la antesala del éxito. Expone ante sus colegas dos trozos de pavo con una rebanada de pan en medio. Todos rechazan su obra salvo David Hume, que presiente la inminencia de algo grandioso y le alienta a seguir.
Enardecido por la amistad del filósofo, vuelve a su trabajo con renovado vigor.

El Conde de Sandwich con horas restando la vitalidad de su propuesta número catorce con David Hume (un retrato de la época compuesto duramente más grabado por entonces que los personajes no aparecen en nada)

1750 en primavera, expone tres trozos consecutivos de jamón, uno encima de otro, y hace una demostración que sólo despierta cierto interés en círculos intelectuales y que pasa desapercibido para el gran público. Tres rebanadas de pan apiladas aumenta su reputación y, aunque todavía no se evidencia un estilo maduro, Voltaire muestra su interés por conocerle.

1751 viajes a Francia donde el filósofo-dramaturgo acaba de lograr interesantes resultados con pan y mahonesa. Los dos hombres se hacen amigos, y se inicia una larga correspondencia que termina abruptamente cuando a Voltaire se le acaban los sellos postales.

1758 su creciente aceptación entre los manipuladores de la opinión pública hace que la Reina le encargue "algo especial" con motivo de un almuerzo con el embajador de **España**. **Trabaja día y noche** experimentando con cientos de posibilidades y, por fin, a las 16 horas 17 minutos del 27 de abril de 1758, crea la obra que consiste en varias tajadas de jamón cubiertas, por encima y por abajo, por dos rebanadas de pan de centeno. En un golpe de inspiración, adorna la obra con mostaza. Es el éxito inmediato, y queda encargado para el resto del año de los almuerzos del sábado.

She wanted "something special"!

—Ella (la Reina) quería "algo especial"!

servírlas con panecillos, una idea que deleita al conde que, más tarde, dice del autor de *Fausto*: "Este Goethe es un gran tipo". Estas palabras deleitan a Goethe, aunque al año siguiente los dos hombres rompen su relación por una desavenencia en torno a los conceptos de crudo, medio hecho y hecho.

1790 en una exposición retrospectiva de su obra celebrada en Londres, sufre un súbito ataque de dolores en el pecho, y se supone una muerte inminente. pero se recupera lo suficiente para supervisar la construcción de un monumento al sandwich de barra promovido por un grupo de talentosos seguidores. Su inauguración en Italia produce serios disturbios y allí permanece incomprendido salvo por unos pocos críticos.

1760 cosecha un éxito tras otro creando "sandwiches", como se los denomina en su honor, con roast-beef, pollo, lengua y casi cualquier fiambre concebible. No satisfecho con repetir fórmulas ya tratadas, busca nuevas ideas y elabora el sandwich-combinado por el cual recibe la Orden de la Jarretera.

1769 en su residencia de campo, recibe la visita de los hombres más ilustres del siglo: Haydn, Kant, Rousseau y Ben Franklin se detienen en su casa, algunos disfrutando de sus admirables creaciones, otros con pedidos para llevar.

1778 aunque físicamente cansado, todavía investiga nuevas formas y escribe en su diario: "Trabajo hasta altas horas de la noche y tuesto todo lo que encuentro en un esfuerzo por mantener el calor". A fines de ese mismo año, su sandwich abierto de roast-beef caliente provoca un escándalo por su franqueza.

1783 para celebrar su sexagésimo quinto cumpleaños, inventa la hamburguesa y hace giras personales por las grandes capitales del mundo preparando hamburguesas en salas de concierto ante numerosas y agradecidas audiencias. En

1792 cae víctima de un *genu varum* que no puede tratar a tiempo y fallece mientras duerme. Es enterrado en Westminster Abbey, y miles de personas presencian sus funerales. En esa ocasión, el gran poeta alemán Hölderlin resume sus logros con una manifiesta reverencia: "Liberó a la humanidad del almuerzo caliente. Todos estamos en deuda con él".

LA COMPAÑIA GENERAL DE **SANDWICHES**

Menu

HORSD'OEUVRES

Country Ham & Blue Cheese Turnovers
Shrimp Spread
Country Pâté
Cheese Asparagus
Vegetable and Cheese Torte

ENTREES

Lamb Curry
*Spicy cubes of lamb mixed with onions,
mushrooms, peppers and raisins.*
Chicken Oriental
*A unique casserole of chicken, snow peas,
mushrooms, artichokes, water chestnuts,
onions … in a light cream sauce.*
Beef Bourguignon
*A hearty Provincial beef stew flavored with
mushrooms, onions, herbs and red wine.*
Parsley-Sesame Chicken
*A whole chicken breast coated with parsley and
sesame seeds, sautéed in lemon butter. Served
with a shallot sour cream sauce.*
Pasta Salads
*A variety of combinations using vegetables,
chicken and seafood. Changes daily.*
Chicken Salad
*Fresh herbs and homemade mayonnaise make
this one of the best.*

SOUPS&BREADS

Potato Mushroom Soup
Tomato Carrot Soup
French Bread
Whole Wheat Baguettes

DESSERTS

Chocolate Velvet
Gâteau Nanni
Oatmeal Cake
Rum-Fudge Brownies
Carrot Cake
Chocolate Amaretto Truffles
Orange Ice

CATERING

La Pêche offers a
complete catering ser-
vice to accommodate
any size party. In addi-
tion to catering, special
orders are available. We
are glad to satisfy any
gourmet request.

Fresh food is made
daily; call for daily
menus. Any item from
our previous menus is
also available.

SPECIALTIES

Béarnaise Sauce
Poppy Seed Dressing
Mayonnaise
Vinaigrette Salad Dressing, M.F.D.
Fudge Sauce

ENTERTAINING

La Pêche makes entertaining easy: stop by on your
way home from work for your last minute needs.
You can also stop by for a carry-out lunch or let us
drop it by. There is a delivery charge.

la pêche

La Pêche

Gourmet to Go
& Catering
1147 Bardstown Road
Louisville, Ky. 40204
(502) 451-0377

Hours:
Tuesday-Friday
10 until 6
Saturday
10 until 4

Available
daily for
January,
February
& March

48

La Pêche

ADDRESS: Louisville, Kentucky, USA

CHEF: Executive chef: Katherine Cary; chef: Michael Lyles

STYLE OF FOOD: Gourmet takeaway and catering service

DESIGNER (Interior): Will Cary

DESIGNER (Graphics): Walter McCord, Walter McCord Graphic Design, Louisville, Kentucky, USA

DATE OF COMPLETION: 1981

GRAPHIC ELEMENTS: Logo, menus, recipe cards, stationery

The typography of the logo seems to vary from one element to the next, but everything is subservient to the wonderfully executed silhouette drawings.

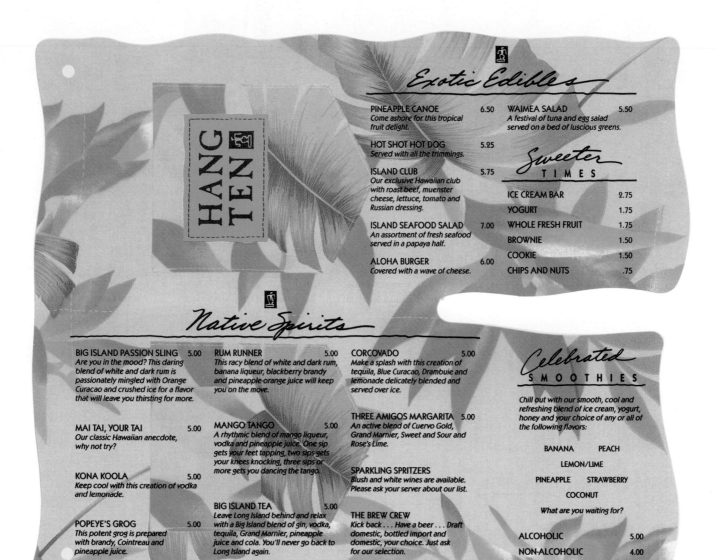

Exotic Edibles

PINEAPPLE CANOE	6.50	
Come ashore for this tropical fruit delight.		
HOT SHOT HOT DOG	5.25	
Served with all the trimmings.		
ISLAND CLUB	5.75	
Our exclusive Hawaiian club with roast beef, muenster cheese, lettuce, tomato and Russian dressing.		
ISLAND SEAFOOD SALAD	7.00	
An assortment of fresh seafood served in a papaya half.		
ALOHA BURGER	6.00	
Covered with a wave of cheese.		

WAIMEA SALAD 5.50
A festival of tuna and egg salad served on a bed of luscious greens.

Sweeter TIMES

ICE CREAM BAR	2.75
YOGURT	1.75
WHOLE FRESH FRUIT	1.75
BROWNIE	1.50
COOKIE	1.50
CHIPS AND NUTS	.75

Native Spirits

BIG ISLAND PASSION SLING 5.00
Are you in the mood? This daring blend of white and dark rum is passionately mingled with Orange Curacao and crushed ice for a flavor that will leave you thirsting for more.

MAI TAI, YOUR TAI 5.00
Our classic Hawaiian anecdote, why not try?

KONA KOOLA 5.00
Keep cool with this creation of vodka and lemonade.

POPEYE'S GROG 5.00
This potent grog is prepared with brandy, Cointreau and pineapple juice.

RUM RUNNER 5.00
This racy blend of white and dark rum, banana liqueur, blackberry brandy and pineapple-orange juice will keep you on the move.

MANGO TANGO 5.00
A rhythmic blend of mango liqueur, vodka and pineapple juice. One sip gets your feet tapping, two sips gets your knees knocking, three sips or more gets you dancing the tango.

BIG ISLAND TEA 5.00
Leave Long Island behind and relax with a Big Island blend of gin, vodka, tequila, Grand Marnier, pineapple juice and cola. You'll never go back to Long Island again.

CORCOVADO 5.00
Make a splash with this creation of tequila, Blue Curacao, Drambuie and lemonade delicately blended and served over ice.

THREE AMIGOS MARGARITA 5.00
An active blend of Cuervo Gold, Grand Marnier, Sweet and Sour and Rose's Lime.

SPARKLING SPRITZERS
Blush and white wines are available. Please ask your server about our list.

THE BREW CREW
Kick back . . . Have a beer . . . Draft domestic, bottled import and domestic, your choice. Just ask for our selection.

Sales tax not included. Please raise flag when you wish to order.

Celebrated SMOOTHIES

Chill out with our smooth, cool and refreshing blend of ice cream, yogurt, honey and your choice of any or all of the following flavors:

BANANA	PEACH
LEMON/LIME	
PINEAPPLE	STRAWBERRY
COCONUT	

What are you waiting for?

ALCOHOLIC	5.00
NON-ALCOHOLIC	4.00

Hang Ten

ADDRESS: Hyatt Regency Hotel, Waikoloa, Hawaii, USA

CHEF: Various

STYLE OF FOOD: American/Californian

NO. OF SEATS: 150

DESIGNER (Graphics): The Associates, Northbrook, Illinois, USA

DATE OF COMPLETION: 1989

GRAPHIC ELEMENTS: Menus, matchboxes, napkins, plates, T-shirts

Exotic bermudas for 'exotic edibles'

OTT (Over the Top)

ADDRESS: London, England

CHEF: Various

STYLE OF FOOD: International

NO. OF SEATS: 100

DESIGNER (Interior): The Architecture Group, London, England

DESIGNER (Graphics): Tim Ellock, London, England

DATE OF COMPLETION: December 1989

GRAPHIC ELEMENTS: Logo, window paintings, T-shirt, menu, flier

The anarchic quality of this solution targets very successfully the younger generation customers and straightaway tells you what type of food to expect.

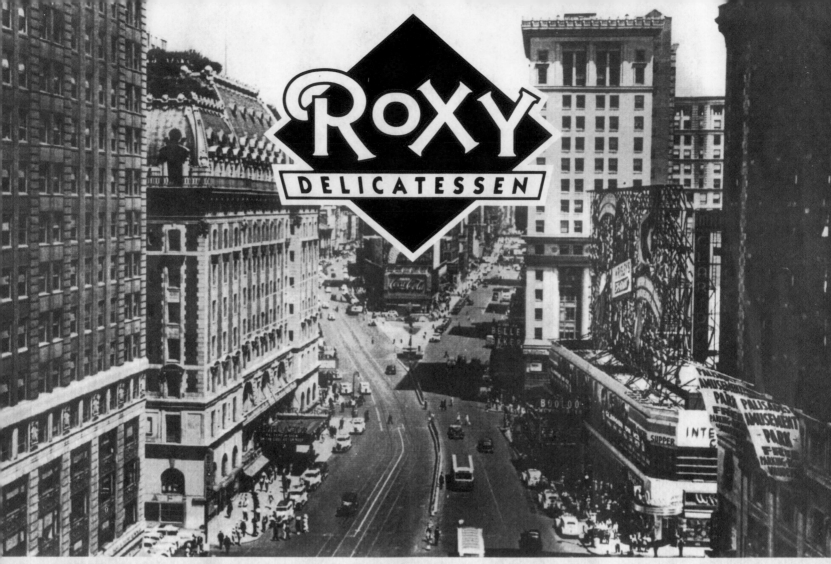

ROXY DELICATESSEN • IN THE TIMES SQUARE TRADITION • 1567 BROADWAY AT 47TH STREET, NEW YORK CITY • TELEPHONE 212/921-3333 • FAX 212/929-9999

Roxy Delicatessen

ADDRESS: New York City, New York, USA

CHEF: Jacob Ben-Moha

STYLE OF FOOD: New York style delicatessen

NO. OF SEATS: 400

DESIGNER: (Interior): Tobin, Parnes, New York City, New York, USA

DESIGNER: (Graphics): Tobin, Parnes, New York City, New York, USA

DATE OF COMPLETION: April 1991

GRAPHIC ELEMENTS: Menu, stationery, logo, tablemats, takeaway bags, signage

In the heart of New York's theatreland, right on Times Square, this restaurant occupies the site of the old Roxy theatre. Even its marquee and graphics owe allegiance to the Great White Way.

TELEPHONE 921-3333
FAX 929-9999

1567 BROADWAY • AT 47TH STREET
NEW YORK CITY

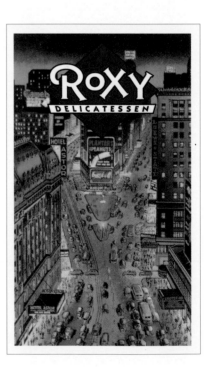

From Our "Gontzeh Megilla" Department

Appetizers
DELICIOUS "MEICHELS" YOU COULD KVELL FROM

Our Fresh-Made-Daily Gefuilte Fish....5.45
Served with lettuce, tomato and horseradish
Stuffed Cabbage....5.95
Chopped Chicken Liver....4.95
"Kishka": Stuffed Derma....5.50
"Pacha": Jellied Calf's Feet....5.95
Individual Can of Tuna, Salmon or Boneless/Skinless Sardines....6.45
Smoked Nova Scota Salmon....6.95
Served with cream cheese
Smoked Lake Sturgeon....6.95
Served with lettuce, tomato and onion
Smoked Whitefish....6.95
Served with lettuce, tomato and onion
"Latkes": 2 Potato Pancakes....5.25
Served with sour cream or apple sauce
Knockwurst on a Bun....4.95
Served with French fries
Foot-long Hot Dog on a Bun....4.95
Served with French fries

Soups
MADE FRESH DAILY "GRANDMA" STYLE

Mushroom Barley....3.25
Matzoh Ball....4.25
Kreplach....[illegible]
Consommé with Noodle Kasha or Rice..3.50
From Russia With Love:
Cold or Hot Borscht....3.95
Served with sour cream
With boiled potato 1.00 additional
Onion Soup au Gratin....3.95

ASK ABOUT OUR SOUPS OF THE DAY 3.50

Entrees
SERVED WITH CHOICE OF TWO:
Mushroom Barley, Kasha Varnishkas, Mashed Potato, Baked Potato, Rice, Vegetable of the Day, Cream of Spinach or French Fries

Pepper Steak....11.45
Corned Beef and Cabbage....10.45
Roast Brisket of Beef with Gravy....11.45
Hungarian Beef Goulash....10.95
"Kishka": Stuffed Derma....10.95
Mixed Platter....13.95
Meatball, derma and stuffed cabbage
Hungarian Stuffed Cabbage....10.45
Pot Roast with Beef Gravy....11.45
Meat Loaf with Beef Gravy....9.95
Roast Beef wth Gravy....11.95

SERVED WITHOUT ACCOMPANIMENTS:
(Who needs more?)

"Flanken": Boiled Beef in the Pot....11.95
With matzoh ball, vegetable and noodles
Potted Meat Balls....9.95
With spaghetti and tomato sauce

From The Broadway Grill
SERVED WITH CHOICE OF TWO:
Mushroom Barley, Kasha Varnishkas, Mashed Potato, Baked Potato, Rice, Vegetable of the Day, Cream of Spinach or French Fries

Broiled Roumanian Karnatzl....12.95
Broiled Roumanian Tenderloin Steak..13.95
1 Lb. Broiled Chopped Sirloin Steak..12.95
Served with sauteed onions
1 Lb. Prime Rib Steak
Broiled to Your Liking....15.95
Broiled Steak Liver....9.95
Served with sauteed onions
Broiled Half Spring Chicken....10.45
Broiled BBQ Ribs....12.45
Broiled T-Bone Steak....15.95
Char-broiled Canadian Baby Back Ribs..12.95
Broiled Chicken Liver a la Dutch....9.95
Served with peppers, onion & gravy
Broiled BBQ Breast of Chicken....12.95

Poultry
SERVED WITH CHOICE OF TWO:
Mushroom Barley, Kasha Varnishkas, Mashed Potato, Baked Potato, Rice, Vegetable of the Day, Cream of Spinach or French Fries

Fried Chicken In The Basket....10.95
Broiled or Roasted Half Spring Chicken..10.95
Half Stuffed Roasted Chicken....12.45
Half BBQ Chicken....11.95
Made with our special sauce
Braised Turkey Wing....9.95
[illegible]
Roasted Turkey....11.95
Served with cranberry sauce
"Schnitzel":
Fried Boneless Breast of Chicken....11.95

Our Famous Chicken In The Pot
Made the old fashioned way:
Noodles, vegetables and matzoh ball only
11.95

Fisherman's Favorite Catch
SERVED WITH CHOICE OF TWO:
Mushroom Barley, Kasha Varnishkas, Mashed Potato, Baked Potato, Rice, Vegetable of the Day, Cream of Spinach or French Fries

Broiled Salmon Steak....14.95
Broiled Fillet of Sole Almonde....11.95
Baked Carp - Hot or Cold....11.95
Halibut Steak - Broiled or Baked....13.95
Baked Red Snapper Fillet....11.95
Fresh Tuna Steak - Broiled or Baked..12.95

Welcome to the Roxy - good food, good people and a place to hang your hat almost any time of the night or day.

ROXY DELICATESSEN

We're bringing back the best of a tradition of delicious food from the days when guys and dolls strolled down old Broadway. Enjoy.

Platters To Plotz From

Salad Platters
NO SKIMPY DIET SALADS BUT A REAL MEAL THAT WON'T LEAVE YOU FROM HUNGER

Fresh White Meat Chicken Salad....9.25
Served with potato salad, cole slaw, lettuce, tomato & radishes
White Meat Tuna Salad....9.25
Served with potato salad, cole slaw, lettuce, tomato & radishes
Chef's Salad....10.95
Turkey, tongue, ham, imported Swiss, boiled eggs, alfalfa sprouts, lettuce, tomato, cucumber & radishes
Greek Salad....10.95
Lettuce, tomato, cucumber, scallions olives, feta cheese & grape leaves
Novie Platter....12.95
[illegible] bagel, Bermuda onion, lettuce, tomato, radishes & capers with lemon
Egg Salad....7.45
Served with potato salad, cole slaw, lettuce, tomato & radishes
Individual Can:
Tuna, Salmon or Skinless Sardines....8.45
Served with hard boiled egg, potato salad, cole slaw, lettuce, tomato & radishes
Chopped Chicken Liver....8.95
Served with hard boiled egg, potato salad, cole slaw, lettuce, tomato & radishes
Shrimp Salad....12.95
Served with potato salad, cole slaw, lettuce, tomato & radishes
Whitefish Salad....10.95
Served with potato salad, cole slaw, lettuce, tomato, radishes & Bermuda onion
Smoked Lake Sturgeon....12.95
Served with potato salad, cole slaw, lettuce, tomato, radishes, Bermuda onion & lemon
Smoked Whitefish....11.95
Served with potato salad, cole slaw, lettuce, tomato, radishes, Bermuda onion & lemon
Gefuilte Fish....10.95
Served with potato salad, lettuce, tomato, radishes & garnished carrots
Pickled Herring....8.95
Served with sour cream, lettuce, tomato, Bermuda onion & radishes

Super Giant Smoked Fish Platter For Two
NOVA SCOTIA SALMON, LAKE STURGEON, WHITEFISH AND SMOKED SABLE
Served with cream cheese, 2 giant bagles, lettuce, tomato, Bermuda onion, capers, radishes & lemon
18.95

Three-Egg And Omelette Combinations
SERVED WITH TOAST OR BASKET OF BREAD AND CHOICE OF FRENCH FRIES OR HOME FRIES

Three Eggs, Your Way....5.45
Jumbo Franks & Eggs....6.95
Beef, Salami or Bologna & Eggs....6.95
Nova Scotia Lox & Eggs....7.95
Corned Beef Hash & Eggs....7.95
Bacon & Eggs....6.95
Pork Sausage & Eggs....6.95
Canadian Bacon & Eggs....7.95
Broiled English Kipper & Eggs....10.45
Boiled or Poached Eggs....5.45
Corned Beef, Pastrami, or Tongue Omelette....8.95
Lake Sturgeon & Onion Omelette....8.95
Matzo Brie....6.95
Fried matzo, pancake style or scrambled
Mushroom Omelette....8.95
Western Omelette....6.95
Spanish Omelette....6.95
Swiss or American Cheese Omelette..7.45
Onion Omelette....6.95

Combination Deli Platters
HOT CUTS, COLD CUTS - BUT NEVER ANY SHORT CUTS

Hot Assorted Cold Cuts....13.95
Choice of 5 meats
Salami & Bologna....9.95
With potato salad
Sliced White Meat Turkey....10.95
With potato salad
Sliced Tongue....10.95
With potato salad
Hot Corned Beef....11.95
With potato salad
2 Foot Long All Beef Franks....9.95
Boiled or broiled
With baked beans & sauerkraut
Roast Beef....11.95
With potato salad
Pastrami & Corned Beef....12.95
With potato salad

Kine-ahora, What A Sandwich

Triple Sky Rockets
TAKE ONE BITE, YOU'LL BE IN HEAVEN

Turkey, Tongue & Chopped Liver....11.95
Served with cole slaw, Russian dressing & onions
Hot Pastrami, Salami & Tongue....12.95
Served with deli mustard & relish
Hot Corned Beef, Tongue & Turkey.12.95
Served with deli mustard & Russian dressing
Chopped Liver, Pastrami, & Imported Swiss....12.50
Served with cole slaw & Russian dressing
Brisket of Beef, Pastrami & Corned Beef....12.95
Served with deli mustard & cole slaw
Turkey, Roast Beef & Tongue....12.95
Served with Bermuda onion, lettuce and tomato
Club Triple Decker BLT....9.95
BACON, LETTUCE & TOMATO
Served with cole slaw & Russian dressing
Club Chicken Decker....8.95
CHICKEN SALAD, CRISP BACON, LETTUCE & TOMATO
Served with cole slaw & Russian dressing
Hard Boiled Egg & Chopped Liver....9.95
Served with Bermuda onion, lettuce & tomato
Tongue, Corned Beef & Salami....11.95
Served with cole slaw & Russian dressing

From Our Carving Board
OPEN WIDE AND SAY AHHHH!

Hot Corned Beef....7.95
Hot Pastrami....7.95
Center Cut Tongue....7.95
Tip Tongue Extra Lean....8.25
All Beef Salami....6.95
Dry Salami....7.95
Chopped Liver....6.95
Chopped Egg Salad....4.25
Hot Brisket of Beef....7.95
Rolled Beef....7.95
Meat Ball....6.95
Roast Beef (Rare)....7.95
Bologna....6.25
Baked Virginia Ham....7.45
Boiled Ham....6.25
Whitefish Salad....7.45
B.L.T.....5.95
Meat Loaf....6.95
Liverwurst....6.95
Sliced Steak....7.95
White Meat Tuna....6.95
White Chicken Salad....6.25
Tuna-melt....7.45
Shrimp Salad....7.95

ALL OF THE ABOVE SERVED WITH LETTUCE
Large roll or bagel .50 extra
Sliced tomato .75 extra • Cheese 1.50 extra

Hot Open Faced
[illegible]

Roast Turkey with Cranberry Sauce..10.95
Roast Brisket of Beef with Gravy....10.95
Served with lettuce & tomato
Pot Roast with Gravy....10.95
Beef Tongue....8.95
Served with deli mustard & cole slaw

The Reuben
A mixed grilled assortment built high with corned beef, imported Swiss cheese and sauerkraut
10.95

Fish
Broiled Fillet of Flounder....6.45
Broiled Fillet of Halibut....7.95
Fried Fillet of Flounder....[illegible]
Herring, Lettuce, Tomato & Onion....7.95
Nova Scotia, Lettuce, Tomato & Onion..9.95
Smoked Whitefish, Lettuce, Tomato & Onion....6.95
Lake Sturgeon on Bagel....9.95

ALL OF THE ABOVE SERVED WITH LETTUCE
Large roll or bagel .50 extra
Sliced tomato .75 extra • Cheese 1.50 extra

Cheese
Sweet Muenster....4.95
American....4.95
[illegible]
Jarlsberg....5.95
Grilled Swiss....5.25
Grilled Muenster....5.25
Melted American....4.95
Cream Cheese & Jelly....3.25

ALL OF THE ABOVE SERVED WITH LETTUCE
Large roll or bagel .50 extra
Sliced tomato .75 extra • Bacon 2.00 extra

Traditional
NOVA SCOTIA WITH CREAM CHEESE ON LARGE TOASTED BAGEL
With lettuce, tomato & Bermuda onion
10.95
2.00 EXTRA FOR SHARING

Twin Family
TWIN JUNIOR ROLLS WITH A CHOICE OF 2 MIXES:
Hot Corned Beef, Pastrami, Turkey, Tongue, Brisket of Beef or Chopped Liver
9.95
1.50 EXTRA PER ADDITIONAL MIX

Smorgasborg Quads
4 JUNIOR ROLLS
Individually Stuffed with Corned Beef, Chopped Liver, Tuna Salad and Chicken Salad
Served with red onion, lettuce, tomato & sweet peppers
16.95

From Our "Big-Tsimmis" Department

Burger Lover's Choice
ROXY'S FAMOUS BEEF BURGER GROUND DAILY
Pure Lean Half-Pound Burgers Served With Lettuce, Tomato, Onion And French Fries

Burger DeLuxe....6.45
American Cheese Burger....7.45
Swiss Burger....7.95
Bacon Burger....7.95
Bacon Cheese Burger....8.95
Corned Beef Burger....8.95
Pastrami Burger....8.95
Pizza Burger....8.95

FOR THE EXTRA LOVER
One Pound Double Beef Burger
9.95

HALF-POUND BURGER ON A BUN
Served with lettuce, tomato & pickles
5.75

Waist Watchers
YEARS AGO DELIS HAD SIGNS "WATCH YOUR COAT" NOW EVERYBODY'S WATCHING WAISTS

Nude 8 Ounce Burger....8.95
Served with cottage cheese and peach half on a bed of lettuce
Broiled Strips of Chicken Breast....9.95
Served with cottage cheese and peach half on a bed of lettuce

On The Side
SOMETIMES A COUPLE OF SIDES COULD BE ENOUGH ALREADY

"Latkis": 2 Potato Pancakes....2.45
French Fried Potatoes....2.25
Fried Onion Rings....2.75
Oven Baked Beans....2.10
Fresh Vegetable of the Day....2.25
Baked Potato....2.25
Mashed Potatoes....2.25
Egg, Barley & Mushroom....2.25
Kasha Varnishkas....2.25
Potato or Kasha Knishes....2.75
Creamed Spinach....2.25
Rice....2.25
Hot Cherry Peppers....2.25
Large Sweet Red Pepper....2.25
Ripe Black Olives....1.95
Bacon....2.45
Sausages....2.45
Cream Cheese....2.25
Sliced Tomatoes....1.75
Sliced Tomatoes & Lettuce....2.25
House Salad....2.50
Potato Kugel....3.25
"Luchshen": Noodle Kugel....3.25
"Kishka": Derma with Gravy....3.95

New York Dairy
IN OLD TIMES SQUARE YOU GOT FRESH WAITERS WITH THE FRESH DAIRY
TODAY ROXY'S DAIRY COMES WITH NICE WAITERS

Our Own Home Made Blintzes:
Cheese, Blueberry, Strawberry or Cherry....7.95
Served with choice of sour cream or apple sauce
Side Order of Fresh Fruit....3.45
Pirogen, Fried or Boiled....7.95
Served with sour cream & fried onion
"Latkis": 3 Potato Pancakes....7.95
Served with choice of sour cream or apple sauce
Challah French Toast....6.95
Served with syrup & jelly
Fresh Fruit & Cottage Cheese with Jello..8.95
Half Cantaloupe with Cottage Cheese5.25
Half Grapefruit....2.25
Bananas & Fresh Strawberries....6.95
Served with sour cream
Diet Bowl....7.95
Fresh vegetables with cottage cheese

ALL MAJOR CREDIT CARDS ACCEPTED

DELI MARKET - TO GO

HOME AND OFFICE DELIVERY

ASK FOR OUR CATERING MENU

PRIVATE DINING ROOM AVAILABLE FOR PARTIES OR BANQUETS UP TO 200 SEATS

OPEN 7 DAYS - 6AM TO 3AM
BREAKFAST SERVED 6AM TO 11AM

2.00 EXTRA FOR SHARING
GO AHEAD, THERE'S PLENTY.

Roxy Delicatessen continued over page

TC Eggington's

ADDRESS: Mesa, Arizona, USA

CHEF: Dean Delgado

STYLE OF FOOD: Brunch and creative egg dishes

NO. OF SEATS: 120 plus 30 patio seats

DESIGNER (Interior): Dwayne Lewis Architects

DESIGNER (Graphics): Richardson or Richardson,
Phoenix, Arizona, USA

DATE OF COMPLETION: November 1985

GRAPHIC ELEMENTS: Matchboxes, menus, business
cards, bills, signage, jam labels, table tents, mugs,
takeaway menus

The best bit of this restaurant identity is the use of
real chicken wire on the menus.

Fat Boy's Diner

ADDRESS: London, England

CHEF: Various

STYLE OF FOOD: All-American diner

NO. OF SEATS: 42

DESIGNER (Graphics): Classic Diners of America Ltd, London, England

DATE OF COMPLETION: 1991

GRAPHIC ELEMENTS: Disposable plates, cola cups, coffee cups, fries pack, menu, postcards, napkins

Mark Yates first got the idea for this chain of authentic 1940s/1950s diners when he saw a 'for sale' ad in a Los Angeles newspaper. He immediately telephoned to make an offer, and flew over there the next day to clinch the deal: before he'd never even heard of an American diner. Now he has had six shipped over to the UK: this one stands in an old bomb site in the centre of London's Covent Garden.

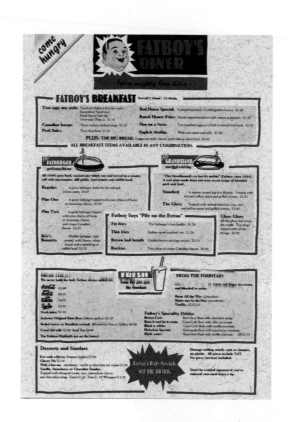

1163 24TH STREET • DES MOINES, IOWA 50311 • (515) 277-3647 • (515) 277-DOGS

1163 24TH STREET • DES MOINES, IOWA 50311 • (515) 277-3647 • (515) 277-DOGS

Chicago Dog & Deli

ADDRESS: Des Moines, Iowa, USA

STYLE OF FOOD: Deli-style hotdogs

NO. OF SEATS: 85

DESIGNER (Graphics): John Sayles, Sayles Graphic
Design, Des Moines, Iowa, USA

DATE OF COMPLETION: 1900

GRAPHIC ELEMENTS: Logo, menu

Conveniently located in 'Dog Town' according to
the menu, which includes hot dog, jumbo dog and
chilli dog: note the ketchup and mustard colours;
even the telephone number is canine.

Executive Surf Club

ADDRESS: Corpus Christi, Texas, USA

CHEF: Rey Vargas

STYLE OF FOOD: Burgers and beer

NO. OF SEATS: 100

DESIGNER (Interior): Bright & Dykemas

DESIGNER (Graphics): The Bradford Lawton Design Group, San Antonio, Texas, USA

DATE OF COMPLETION: 1990

GRAPHIC ELEMENTS: Poster, Surf's Up T-shirt

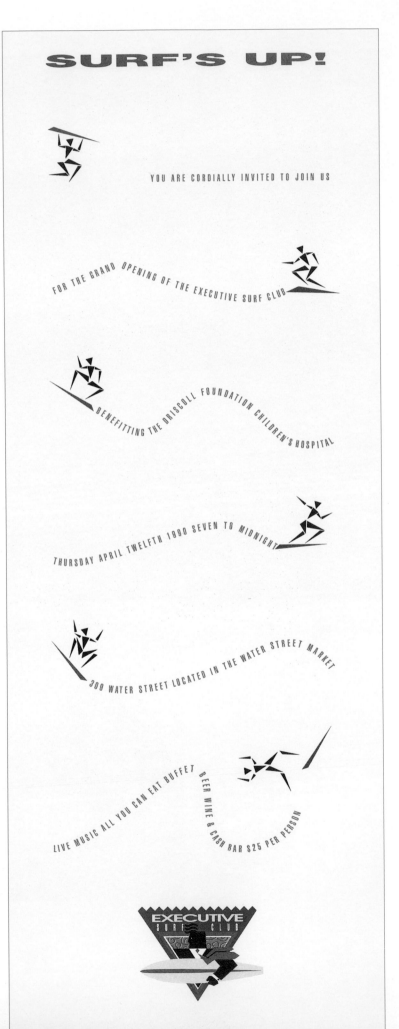

Sky Diver

ADDRESS: Jean, Nevada, USA

CHEF: Dennis Woods

STYLE OF FOOD: Continental/Barbecue

NO OF SEATS: 125

DESIGNER (Interior): Yates/Silverman

DESIGNER (Graphics): Dick Witt, The Kenyon Press,
Hawthorne, California, USA; illustrator:
Pamela Mower-Conner

DATE OF COMPLETION: 1990

GRAPHIC ELEMENTS: Menu

Fun for kids and well executed of its kind; it must
be almost the same size as most of its young diners.

Tibidabo

ADDRESS: Chain of four restaurants in an
amusement park complex, Barcelona, Spain

CHEF: Inma Buxeres, Juan Canas

STYLE OF FOOD: Fast food

NO. OF SEATS: Total in all four venues: 1132

DESIGNER (Interior): Various architects

DESIGNER (Graphics): Carlos Rolando, CR
Communication & Design Services SA, Barcelona,
Spain

DATE OF COMPLETION: June 1989

GRAPHIC ELEMENTS: Logo, menus, matchboxes

Of the four solutions within this complex,
I particularly like the Self O No Self Logo.

Aubépain

ADDRESS: Chain throughout Paris, France; also at
Marignane, Toulouse, Grenoble, Nantes, Rouen

STYLE OF FOOD: Fast food and snacks

NO. OF SEATS: 30–50

DESIGNER (Interior): Gérard Moratille/GBGM, Paris,
France

DESIGNER (Graphics): Ludovic Lemoine/GBGM,
Paris, France

DATE OF COMPLETION: January 1991

GRAPHIC ELEMENTS: Place mats, napkin, cups

A very 'French' solution, clean, neat and nicely
executed with none of the cheapness usually
associated with fast food.

STARTERS

CHILLED SOUP- Cucumber, orange & mint £1.50
DEEP FRIED MUSHROOMS with Boursin Cheese dressing £1.50
HOUSE HORS D'OEUVRES £2.25   MELON in Season £2.25
BALTIC HERRING with onion, apple & sour cream £2.95
PLATE OF CRUDITE £1.50   HOUSE PATE £1.95
SCOTCH SMOKED SALMON with brown bread £4.75

FISH

GRILLED PLAICE on the bone with lemon butter £3.50
TROUT with mushrooms & shrimp sauce £3.50
FRIED SQUID with Provençale sauce £3.50
FISH PIE with a cheddar cheese crust £2.95
SCOTCH SALMON grilled or poached, Hollandaise sauce £6.95
SCOTCH SALMON SALAD £6.95
DOVER SOLE grilled or Meunière £7.50
MIXED FISH KEBAB with herb sauce, pilaf rice £3.95

VEGETABLES POTATOES SALAD

French Beans 70p   Sauté potatoes 60p
Broccoli 70p   Lyonnaise 60p
Today's Selection 70p   New potatoes 60p

Chef's Special Salad £1.75 / £2.95
Green Salad 95p   Tomato & Onion £1.20
Cucumber with Fresh Dill £1.20

MEAT & POULTRY

PÔT ROAST POUSSIN with garlic & herbs £3.50
ROAST RACK OF LAMB with fresh thyme £5.25
GRILLED SIRLOIN STEAK Bearnaise sauce £7.50
FILLET STEAK with green peppers, brandy & cream £7.75
CALVES LIVER pan-fried with lemon & sage £4.50
ESCALOPE OF VEAL with a mushroom cream sauce £4.95
ROAST DUCK with stem ginger & orange sauce £5.25
STEAK, KIDNEY & MUSHROOM PIE £2.95
CHICKEN & YORK HAM SALAD £3.95

DESSERT FRUIT CHEESE

Passion Fruit Mousse £1.60   Smith's Whiskey Trifle £1.60
Sorbet or Ice Cream £1.25
Profiteroles with Chocolate Sauce £1.60   Gateaux £1.95
Crème Brûlée £1.25   Fresh Fruit Selection £1.95
Cheese Board - Selection £1.95

COFFEE TEA INFUSIONS

COFFEE Filter / Decaffeinated 60p
INFUSIONS: Camomile, Lime, Verbena 90p
TEA: Pure Darjeeling, Assam, Earl Grey, Passion, Florentina

OPEN MONDAY TO SATURDAY - NOON TO MIDNIGHT.
CHEF'S RESTAURANT 32 SHELTON STREET, FIVE DIALS.
COVENT GARDEN, LONDON WC1. LAST ORDERS 11.15pm

A SERVICE CHARGE OF 12½% WILL BE ADDED TO THE BILL.
ALL ITEMS INCLUDE VALUE ADDED TAX. NO ITEMS SUBJECT
TO AVAILABILITY. REGISTRATION 69-370 5138.

FRESH SALADS

SAUTEED SEAFOOD SALAD 6.95
Scallops, shrimp, fresh zucchini & bacon sauteed in white
wine then poured over fresh crisp greens and sprinkled with
jack cheese—Rusty's favorite

PASTA AND CHICKEN SALAD 6.25
Chunks of tender white meat chicken tossed with chilled
shell pasta, garden fresh vegetables, provolone cheese,
and Italian dressing.

PASTA AND SHRIMP SALAD 7.25
Chilled shell pasta, bay shrimp, fresh broccoli, zucchini, carrots,
bell pepper and tomatoes all mixed with Italian dressing
and provolone cheese.

FRESH SPINACH SALAD 5.25
Avocado, chopped egg, real bacon—and more!

CHILLED SEAFOOD LOUIES
with Crab 7.95   with shrimp 6.95

MAC'S LUNCH 4.95
A bowl of Rusty's clam chowder and a tossed green or fresh
spinach salad with choice   of dressings:
Homemade blue cheese,
red raspberry vinaigrette or
chilled Italian bacon.

Mainstream Restaurants

The work in this section reflects what is happening around the world. These projects have been grouped together because the design and the theme of the restaurants are international even if the food of the name owes something to regional or ethnic inspiration.

Eureka

ADDRESS: Los Angeles, California, USA

CHEF: Wolfgang Puck and Jody Denton

STYLE OF FOOD: 'Anything that goes with a beer'; an eclectic blend of Asian, Latin and European cuisines, an expansion of 'California Cuisine'

NO. OF SEATS: 180

DESIGNER (Interior): Barbara Lazaroff, Imaginings Interior Design Inc, Los Angeles, California, USA

DESIGNER (Graphics): Bright & Associates, Santa Monica, California, USA

DATE OF COMPLETION: 1990

GRAPHIC ELEMENTS: Matchboxes, menu, napkins, sweatshirts, baseball caps, flags, umbrellas, matchbooks, beer bottle labels

This logo – like a monogram on a cricketer's cap, or a family crest – combines all the letters of the name. It is incorporated within a complicated design that precisely emulates a beer label and is applied to dozens of in-house and giveaway items.

APPETIZERS

GULF OYSTERS ON THE HALF SHELL
ONE DOZEN..........5.50   HALF DOZEN..........2.95

"YOU PEEL'EM" SHRIMP................4.95
Boiled and chilled. Priced by the quarter pound.

EMBROCHETTE................4.75
Four gulf oysters, each wrapped in shrimp,
then bacon-wrapped, and deep fried without batter.

PICAYUNE................5.75
Five large shrimp, peeled, oven broiled in a spicy Cajun-style sauce.
Served with freshly baked bread for dunking.

SOFT SHELL CRAB................7.25
Two soft shell crabs, served in season. Battered in tempura.

SEAFOOD GUMBO
Served over rice.
BOWL ....3.75   CUP..........2.50

CALDO XOCHITL
A South Texas favorite. A substantial Mexican soup
of chicken, garden vegetables and rice.
BOWL................3.50   CUP..........2.25

SEAFOOD QUESADILLAS................4.95
Grilled flour tortillas filled with grilled fish, shrimp and Monterrey
Jack cheese. Served with guacamole, sour cream and pico de gallo.

BAKED OYSTERS

OYSTERS ROCKEFELLER................5.50
Six freshly shucked oysters baked with chopped herbed spinach
and crumbled bacon. Generously topped with melted
Monterrey Jack cheese.

OYSTERS CASINO................5.50
Six freshly shucked oysters baked with a topping of bacon,
bread crumbs, celery, butter and lemon.

OYSTERS PARMAGIANA................5.25
Six freshly shucked oysters baked with a topping of parmesan cheese,
red bell pepper, bread crumbs, butter and white wine.

OYSTERS COMBINATION................5.50
Two of each of the above.

SPECIALTIES
All specialties include freshly baked bread,
creamery butter, rice pilaf, and today's fresh vegetable.

BLACKENED FRESH CATCH................MARKET PRICE
Today's blackboard special coated with our own blend
of nine spices and herbs, and blackened on the griddle.

PICAYUNE PLATTER................10.95
Seven large shrimp, peeled, oven broiled and flavored
with a spicy Cajun-style sauce.

EMBROCHETTE PLATTER................10.50
Eight gulf oysters each wrapped in shrimp, then bacon-wrapped
and deep fried without batter.

FRESH CATCH NUECES................MARKET PRICE
Today's fresh fillet, sautéed and topped with gulf shrimp
and blue crab meat in a rich browned butter sauce.

BLACKENED TENDERLOIN................11.50
An 8-ounce filet of beef coated with our own blend
of nine spices and herbs then blackened on the griddle.

STEAK & SHRIMP................12.95
An 8-ounce USDA Choice ribeye, mesquite grilled, and served
with four large fried shrimp.

SHRIMP-K-BOB................11.50
Eight large shrimp skewered with onion, bell pepper and
mushrooms, marinated and mesquite grilled.

TENDERLOIN................10.95
An 8-ounce filet, bacon-wrapped and grilled over mesquite.

MESQUITE CHICKEN................7.95
An 8-ounce chicken breast marinated and grilled over mesquite.

SALADS

GRILLED CHICKEN CAESAR SALAD................5.75
A five ounce skinless chicken breast marinated and grilled,
served over a Caesar salad tossed with our special dressing.

PASTA & SHRIMP SALAD................4.95
Spiral pasta and sautéed shrimp mixed with a creamy tarragon dressing.

SOUP & SALAD................4.95
A bowl of Caldo Xochitl and a tossed salad.

GULF SHRIMP SALAD................6.25
Boiled shrimp in a lemon mustard dressing topped
with avocado and tomato.

BLACKBOARD
Our blackboard menu best demonstrates our commitment to
freshness. Changing constantly according to the availability of fresh
seafood in the coastal market place, it reflects the wide variety
of fish species populating our gulf waters and beyond.

DEEP FRIED
All deep fried dishes include freshly baked bread,
creamery butter, rice pilaf and today's fresh vegetable.

GULF SAMPLER................12.95
Three large shrimp, four gulf oysters, one crab cake
and one four ounce fillet of fish.

SHRIMP & OYSTERS................10.50
Four large shrimp and four gulf oysters.

NO. 3 COMBINATION................11.50
Three fried shrimp, three fried oysters and three embrochette.

LARGE GULF SHRIMP
Butterflied and lightly battered in flour and bread crumbs.
SMALL ORDER (5).................2.75
LARGE ORDER (7)................10.50

DEEP FRIED GULF OYSTERS
Fresh from the Gulf, lightly battered in corn flour.
SMALL ORDER (7)................6.75
LARGE ORDER (10)................8.95

BLUE CRAB CAKES (3)................9.50
Gulf style crab cakes, made with fresh blue crab meat
in a bread crumb coating.

SOFT SHELL CRAB (3)................13.95
Served in season, battered in tempura.

SANDWICHES
Served with french fries.

OYSTER LOAF................5.25
Fried oysters on a french roll with creole tartar sauce.

SHRIMP PO'BOY................5.25
Fried shrimp on a french roll with creole tartar sauce.

WATER STREET BURGER................4.50
One third-pound freshly ground patty grilled over mesquite,
served on a freshly baked onion roll with or without cheese.

Side Orders
Substitutions are gladly accepted

FRENCH FRIES................1.50
FRESH VEGETABLE OF THE DAY................1.50
RICE PILAF................1.50
HOUSE SALAD................1.50
BAKED POTATO................2.25
AS A SUBSTITUTE.................95

BEVERAGES

ICE TEA.................95
COFFEE/HOT TEA.................95
COKE, DIET COKE, SPRITE.................95
ARTESIA CON LIME................1.00
MILK................1.00
ICE WATER SERVED UPON REQUEST

CHILDREN'S MENU
Designed for children 12 and under.

WATER STREET BURGER................4.50
One third-pound freshly ground patty grilled over mesquite,
served on a freshly baked onion roll with or without cheese.

CRAB CAKE AND FRIES................3.25
One gulf-style crab cake and fries. (Extra crab cake 1.85 each)

KID SHRIMP & FRIES................4.25
Seven child-size shrimp and fries.

FRESH CATCH................5.25
A 4-ounce fillet deep fried or mesquite grilled and served with french fries.

DESSERTS

NEW ORLEANS BREAD PUDDING
WITH BOURBON SAUCE................2.50
HOT FUDGE BROWNIE WITH
VANILLA BLUEBELL ICE CREAM................2.25
PRALINE CHEESECAKE................2.75
BUNUELO BOWL................2.75

A SPECIAL NOTE
If at all possible, we will be happy to accommodate any special
preparation requests of menu items. Ask your server for assistance.
We advise our guests to be prudent in their alcohol consumption.
We further remind you of the dangers of driving while under the influence
of alcohol. It is our policy to restrict the sale of alcohol to anyone who,
in our opinion, may present a danger to themselves or others.
We appreciate your understanding.
If our service pleases you, allow us to add 15% gratuity
to groups of eight or more. Thank you.

Water Street Oyster Bar

ADDRESS: San Antonio and Fort Worth, Texas, USA

CHEF: Rey Vargas

STYLE OF FOOD: Seafood

NO. OF SEATS: 185 (San Antonio) and 150 (Fort Worth)

DESIGNER (Interior): Bright & Dykemas

DESIGNER (Graphics): The Bradford Lawton Design Group, San Antonio, Texas

DATE OF COMPLETION: 1991

GRAPHIC ELEMENTS: Menus, T-shirts, mural, direct mail shot

Precision typography and a nice illustration that works equally well very large or very small.

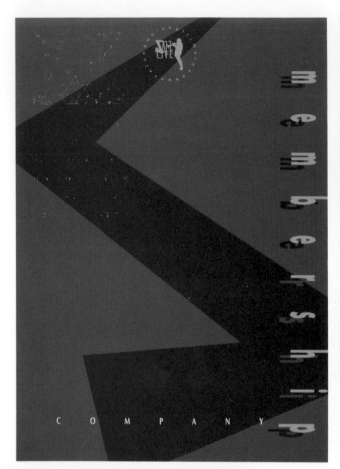

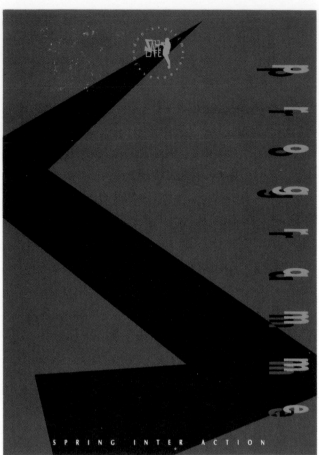

Jazz Cafe

ADDRESS: London, England

CHEF: Barbara Lintzgy and Ian Doel

STYLE OF FOOD: International style wholefood

NO. OF SEATS: 150

DESIGNER (Interior): Chassay Architects, London, England

DESIGNER (Graphics): GIDA Design, London, England

DATE OF COMPLETION: December 1990

GRAPHIC ELEMENTS: Stationery, business cards, programmes, fly posters, logo, calendar, T-shirts

You can almost *hear* the music when you look at these graphics.

Le Pont de la Tour

ADDRESS: London, England

CHEF: David Burke

STYLE OF FOOD: Traditional Eclectic

NO. OF SEATS: 200

DESIGNER (Interior): Sir Terence Conran;
Keith Hobbs

DESIGNER (Graphics): Steve Trimm, RSCG Conran
Design, London, England

DATE OF COMPLETION: September 1991

GRAPHIC ELEMENTS: Stationery, menu

Taking its imagery from the bridge of the same
name, Sir Terence Conran's 'gastrodome' has a
logo that evokes 1930s France. The complex
includes a seafood bar, a grill, a restaurant, a food
store and bakery and a wine shop.

ON THE RIVER BY TOWER BRIDGE

LIZ CARBONI

Le PONT de la TOUR Limited · THE BUTLERS WHARF BUILDING
36d SHAD THAMES · BUTLERS WHARF · LONDON · SE1 2YE
OFFICE 071 403 4455 · FAX 071 403 0267

RESTAURANT · BAR · GRILL · FRUITS de MER · SALON PRIVE · WINE MERCHANT · FOOD STORE · BAKERY
Le PONT de la TOUR Limited   THE BUTLERS WHARF BUILDING
36d SHAD THAMES   BUTLERS WHARF   LONDON   SE1 2YE
OFFICE 071 403 4455   FAX 071 403 0267
REGISTERED IN LONDON Nº 2512932   VAT Nº 548 0197 33

ON THE RIVER BY TOWER BRIDGE

RESTAURANT · BAR · GRILL · FRUITS de MER · SALON PRIVE · WINE MERCHANT · FOOD STORE · BAKERY
Le PONT de la TOUR Limited   THE BUTLERS WHARF BUILDING
36d SHAD THAMES   BUTLERS WHARF   LONDON   SE1 2YE
OFFICE 071 403 4455   FAX 071 403 0267

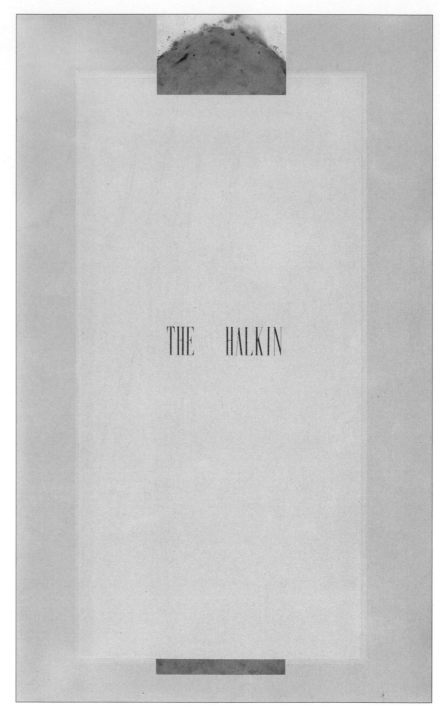

Gualtiero Marchesi at The Halkin

ADDRESS: Halkin Hotel, London, England

CHEF: Stefano Cavallini

STYLE OF FOOD: Italian

NO. OF SEATS: 45

DESIGNER (Interior): Laboratino Associati, Milan, Italy

DESIGNER (Graphics): Gualtiero Marchesi/The Halkin Hotel, London, England

DATE OF COMPLETION: September 1991

GRAPHIC ELEMENTS: Matchboxes, menu, china, silver, linen

Subtle, textural graphics for the restaurant in London's first 'designer' hotel, inspired by the Royalton and the Paramount in New York and La Villa in France.

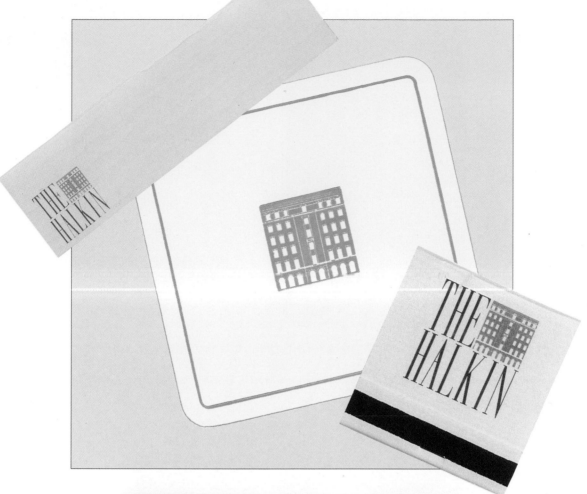

MacArthur Park

ADDRESS: San Francisco, California, USA

CHEF: Roger Greene

STYLE OF FOOD: Innovative American Cuisine

NO. OF SEATS: 200

DESIGNER (Graphics): Morla Design, San Francisco, USA; illustrator Jeanette Aramburu

DATE OF COMPLETION: January 1990

GRAPHIC ELEMENTS: Menu

Planet Hollywood

ADDRESS: New York City, New York, USA

CHEF: David Springett

STYLE OF FOOD: California cuisine

NO. OF SEATS: 220

DESIGNER (Interior): Anton Furst, California, USA

DESIGNER (Graphics): Anton Furst, California, USA

DATE OF COMPLETION: 1991

GRAPHIC ELEMENTS: Logo, menu, placemats, T-shirts, baseball caps, bathrobes

Anton Furst, the set designer from the film Batman also created the setting for this piece of Hollywood in New York. Working with partners Arnold Schwarzenegger, Sylvester Stallone and Bruce Willis, he has borrowed decorative memorabilia from various movies including Robin Hood, Butch Cassidy and the Sundance Kid, the James Bond series and of course Arnie's metal skeleton from Terminator. As part of the pre-opening launch, logo-adorned T-shirts, baseball caps, leather jackets and even bathrobes were sent to stars such as Madonna, who was photographed jogging in a Planet Hollywood T-shirt. As far as we know, President Bush has not been seen wearing his PH bathrobe . . .

Smith's of Neal Street

ADDRESS: London, England

CHEF: Francis Ageypong

STYLE OF FOOD: English

NO. OF SEATS: 180

DESIGNER (Interior): Christina Smith

DESIGNER (Graphics): Christopher Brown and David Remfry

DATE OF COMPLETION: 1984

GRAPHIC ELEMENTS: Stationery, matchboxes, menus, winelist

Now superseded by a menu that features an illustration of the owner, these original graphics in a wood-cut style of illustration, are still used on some elements of the restaurant's stationery.

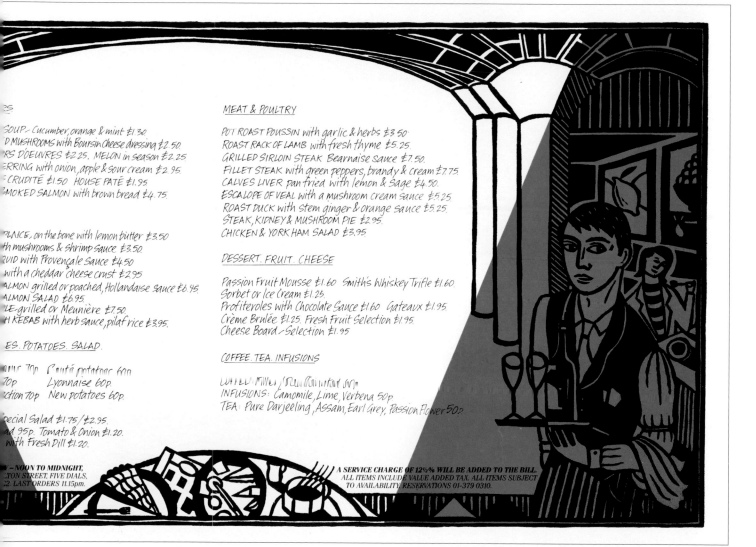

...S

...SOUP - Cucumber, orange & mint £1.30.
...D MUSHROOMS with Boursin Cheese dressing £2.50.
...RS D'OEUVRES £2.25. MELON in season £2.25.
...ERRING with onion, apple & sour cream £2.95.
...E CRUDITÉ £1.50. HOUSE PATÉ £1.95.
...SMOKED SALMON with brown bread £4.75.

...PLAICE, on the bone with lemon butter £3.50.
...th mushrooms & shrimp sauce £3.50.
...QUID with Provençale sauce £4.50.
...with a cheddar cheese crust £2.95.
...ALMON grilled or poached, Hollandaise sauce £6.95.
...ALMON SALAD £6.95.
...LE-grilled or Meunière £7.50.
...H KEBAB with herb sauce, pilaf rice £3.95.

...ES. POTATOES. SALAD.

...ANS 70p. Sauté potatoes 60p.
...70p. Lyonnaise 60p.
...ction 70p. New potatoes 60p.

...pecial Salad £1.75 / £2.95.
...ad 95p. Tomato & Onion £1.20.
...with Fresh Dill £1.20.

...Y - NOON TO MIDNIGHT,
...LTON STREET, FIVE DIALS,
...2. LAST ORDERS 11.15pm.

MEAT & POULTRY

POT ROAST POUSSIN with garlic & herbs £3.50.
ROAST RACK OF LAMB with fresh thyme £5.25.
GRILLED SIRLOIN STEAK Bearnaise sauce £7.50.
FILLET STEAK with green peppers, brandy & cream £7.75.
CALVES LIVER pan fried with lemon & sage £4.50.
ESCALOPE OF VEAL with a mushroom cream sauce £5.25.
ROAST DUCK with stem ginger & orange sauce £5.25.
STEAK, KIDNEY & MUSHROOM PIE £2.95.
CHICKEN & YORK HAM SALAD £3.95.

DESSERT. FRUIT. CHEESE

Passion Fruit Mousse £1.60   Smith's Whiskey Trifle £1.60.
Sorbet or Ice Cream £1.25.
Profiteroles with Chocolate Sauce £1.60   Gateaux £1.95.
Crème Brulée £1.25. Fresh Fruit Selection £1.95.
Cheese Board - Selection £1.95

COFFEE. TEA. INFUSIONS

COFFEE/FILTER/Drink/Cappuccino 60p.
INFUSIONS: Camomile, Lime, Verbena 50p.
TEA: Pure Darjeeling, Assam, Earl Grey, Passion Flower 50p.

A SERVICE CHARGE OF 12½% WILL BE ADDED TO THE BILL.
ALL ITEMS INCLUDE VALUE ADDED TAX. ALL ITEMS SUBJECT
TO AVAILABILITY. RESERVATIONS 01-379 0310.

PASSATGE DE LA CONCEPCIÓ 5   08008 BARCELONA   TLF. 487 01 96
OFICINA: ROSSELLÓ 265   08008 BARCELONA   TLF. 218 36 85

El Tragaluz

ADDRESS: Barcelona, Spain

CHEF: Pieter van de Lint and Joan Ferrer

STYLE OF FOOD: International

NO. OF SEATS: 100 plus bars

DESIGNER (Interior): Pepe Cortes and Sandra
Tarruella

DESIGNER (Graphics): Javier Mariscal

DATE OF COMPLETION: 1990

GRAPHIC ELEMENTS: Menu, matchboxes, stationery,
china

This style of lettering as illustration has almost
become Mariscal's trademark. Originally known for
his paintings, his work now extends to shops and
nightclubs and the mascot for the 1992 Olympics
which Barcelona is hosting. The large plate is part
of the table display and not meant for food.

El Tragaluz continued over page

El Tragaluz continued

Kabuto

ADDRESS: Tokyo, Japan

CHEF: Kiyohiko Anzai

STYLE OF FOOD: Japanese, Korean and Thai cuisine

NO. OF SEATS: 100

DESIGNER (Interior): Maria Luisa Rossi and Vincenzo Iavicoli/Iavicoli & Rossi, Florence, Italy

DESIGNER (Graphics): Yuji Takahashi

DATE OF COMPLETION: May 1990

GRAPHIC ELEMENTS: Chopsticks, chopstick rests, napkins, napkin rests, beer coasters, matchboxes, promotional flyers, location maps

'Kabuto' means war-helmet. The large copper helmet-shaped 'lids' on the tables cover the individual cooking facilities. This is a Kaisen-shabu restaurant, a Japanese version of fondue, with fish replacing meat.

Kabuto continued over page

Kabuto continued

Fat Pigs Continental

ADDRESS: Manchester, England

CHEF: Stephen Ribchester

STYLE OF FOOD: International cuisine

NO. OF SEATS: 126

DESIGNER (Interior): Design LSM, London, England

DESIGNER (Graphics): Nikki Hill Graphic Design, London, England

DATE OF COMPLETION: 1990

GRAPHIC ELEMENTS: Menu, stationery, coasters, napkins, T-shirts, matchbooks, badges, baseball caps, balloons, cocktail stirrers

Who could fail to have fun in a restaurant which features this drawing on its menu?

Fat Pigs continued over page

Menu

Fat Pigs continued

17 Church Street Eccles
Manchester M30 0DF
061 789 8080

Managing Director Mark Hurley   Financial Director David Mosey
Registered in England No. 110638 (The Golden Bunny Ltd trading as Fat Pigs Continental)

With Compliments

17 Church Street Eccles
Manchester M30 0DF
061 789 8080

Deals Restaurant Diner

ADDRESS: London, England

CHEF: Tong Jieamtarvorn

STYLE OF FOOD: International

NO. OF SEATS: 180

DESIGNER (Interior): Brian Miller of Brian Miller Designs, London, England

DESIGNER (Graphics): Robin Proctor/Robin Proctor Design Consultancy, London, England

DATE OF COMPLETION: May 1988

GRAPHIC ELEMENTS: Matchboxes, menus, T-shirts

DEALS
RESTAURANT · DINER

HARBOUR YARD
CHELSEA HARBOUR, LONDON SW10 0XD
01-376 3232

DEALS
RESTAURANT · DINER

HARBOUR YARD CHELSEA HARBOUR LONDON SW10
071-376 3232 · 071-352 5887

Blackhawk Grille

ADDRESS: Danville, California, USA

CHEF: Eliot King

STYLE OF FOOD: Californian – Mediterranean

NO. OF SEATS: 200 (150 inside, 50 outside)

DESIGNER (Interior): Eric Engstrom, Barbara Hofling, Jennifer Johanson/Engstrom and Hofling. Corte Madera, California, USA

DESIGNER (Graphics): Rick Tharp, Jean Mogannam, Kim Tomlinson/Tharp Did It, Los Gatos, California, USA

DATE OF COMPLETION: February 1991

GRAPHIC ELEMENTS: Logo, menu, wineboard, cocktail napkins, matchboxes, wine glasses, wine labels, stationery

A major focus of the interior is the display of a classic automobile. The restaurant was named after the community in which it is located and is also a subtle reference to the classic automotive theme; the logotype harks back to that bygone era of automotive history. The Bird adds fun and animation.

95

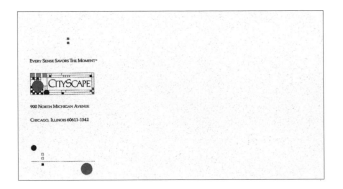

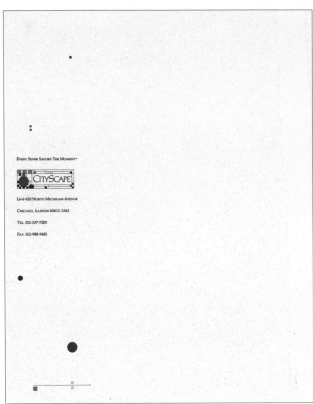

INTERMEZZO

FRESH FRUIT SORBET. 1.50

PASTA

PENNE PASTA
Roasted plum tomatoes, wild mushrooms, mozzarella and red chilies. 5.95
Entree Portion. 10.95

LINGUINE and GOAT CHEESE
Bacon, mushrooms, fried tomatoes and basil juice. 5.95
Entree Portion. 9.95

BOW TIE PASTA
Steamed little neck clams, pea pods, pancetta and garlic herb broth. 6.95
Entree Portion. 11.95

TUBULAR PASTA
Hickory smoked chicken and boursin cheese. 6.95
Entree Portion. 11.95

SPINACH TORTELLINI
Tenderloin tips, mushrooms and tomato cream sauce. 6.95
Entree portion. 11.95

FETTUCINE and SMOKED SALMON
Lemon zest, dill and shallot butter sauce. 6.95
Entree Portion. 12.95

ENTREE

SAUTEED WHITEFISH
Tomatoes, zucchini, yellow squash and eggplant. 13.95

ROASTED BREAST OF CHICKEN
Filled with spinach and scallops, oregano jus. 14.95

PEPPERED MONKFISH
Served on bow tie pasta with red peppers, black olives and pea pods. 15.95

GRILLED BABY SALMON STEAKS
Steamed clams, angel hair pasta and smoked garlic sauce. 16.95

GRILLED MEDALLIONS of BEEF
Fried potatoes and leeks, shallot hollandaise. 17.95

SEARED HAWAIIAN TUNA
Served rare with cucumber radish salad and red radish butter sauce. 18.95

SAUTEED RED SNAPPER
Spicy tomato herb sauce, anaheim pepper and angel hair pasta. 19.95

GRILLED VEAL CHOP
Filled with spinach, sage and tomato, served with polenta. 18.95

APPETIZER

THREE CHEESE LASAGNA
Parmesan, mozzarella and goat cheeses, layered with won tons. 4.95

PAN FRIED RISSOTO CAKE
Melted mozzarella, tomato, garlic and basil. 5.95

CRUNCHY FRIED SHRIMP
Wrapped with Chinese egg noodles, tangy marmalade sauce. 6.95

BAKED PHYLLO PURSES
Filled with seafood, caviar butter sauce. 6.95

GRILLED SEA SCALLOPS
On a potato nest, roasted sesame dressing. 6.95

HOUSE CURED SALMON
Lime cream and assorted caviars. 7.95

CHILLED ROAST VEAL
Chives, radicchio and green peppercorn mayonnaise. 7.95

SOUP

CITYSCAPE CLAM CHOWDER
Light cream chowder flavored with fresh dill. 3.95

SALAD

SEASONAL GREENS
Beet chips, boursin cheese and red wine vinaigrette. 3.95

SMOKED DUCK BREAST
Seasonal greens, quail egg and walnut vinaigrette. 5.95
Entree Portion. 10.95

HAWAIIAN TUNA
Sliced raw, with avocado, bibb lettuce, red onion, tomatoes and lemon soy dressing. 6.95
Entree Portion. 11.95

WARM SEAFOOD SALAD
Shrimp, calamari, bay scallops, mixed greens and parmesan vinaigrette. 8.95

ROASTED SIRLOIN SANDWICH
Tomatoes, avocado and horseradish mayonnaise on pumpernickel. 8.95

CHICKEN SALAD
Fennel, pinenuts, rosemary mayonnaise, warm brioche. 9.95

CHILLED ASPARAGUS and GRILLED SHRIMP
Vegetable vinaigrette. 9.95

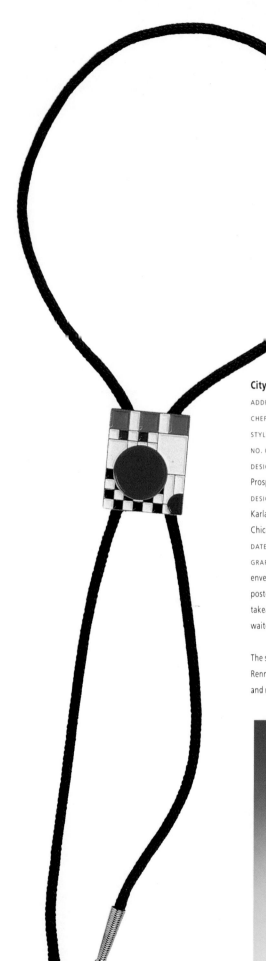

CityScape Restaurant

ADDRESS: Chicago, Illinois, USA

CHEF: Scott Harris and David Friedman

STYLE OF FOOD: American Cuisine

NO. OF SEATS: 180

DESIGNER (Interior): Aumiller Youngquist, Mount Prospect, Illinois, USA

DESIGNER (Graphics): Robert Qually, Holly Thomas, Karla Walusiak and Tim Scott/Qually and Company, Chicago, Illinois, USA

DATE OF COMPLETION: September 1989

GRAPHIC ELEMENTS: Menus, wine list, letterhead, envelopes, business card, gift certificate, postcards/direct mailer, wine bottle labels, takeaway sticker, notepads, bolo tie worn by waiters

The solution seems to be inspired by Charles Rennie Mackintosh and the Vienna Secessionists – and none the worse for that

Arcadia

ADDRESS: New York City, New York, USA

CHEF: Anne Rosenzweig

STYLE OF FOOD: Inventive American

NO. OF SEATS: 65

DESIGNER (Interior): Randy Croxton

DESIGNER (Graphics): Kenneth Kneitel (menu, matchboxes), Paul Davis (mural and wine labels)/Paul Davis Studio, New York City, New York, USA

DATE OF COMPLETION: 1985

GRAPHIC ELEMENTS: Menu, matchboxes, wine labels, cookbook, restaurant cards

Three walls of this small restaurant are covered with a mural by illustrator Paul Davis which depicts an 'Arcadian' landscape in all its seasons.

Tumbledowns

ADDRESS: Cos Cob and Bronxville, New York, USA

CHEF: Terence Considine

STYLE OF FOOD: American/Continental

NO. OF SEATS: 56

DESIGNER (Graphics): Crabshell Design, Stamford, New York, USA

DATE OF COMPLETION: 1990

GRAPHIC ELEMENTS: Menu

This menu is like reading the chef's Last Will & Testament – an impeccable use of Georgian elements.

THE
MENU
offered by
TUMBLEDOWN'S
COS COB
BRONXVILLE

WIT, and HUMOUR.

Who loves not wine, woman and song he's a fool his whole life long.

People ask you for criticism, but only want praise

The worst men often give the best advice.

It ain't over 'til it's over.

The currency of the 1990's is going to be time.

Better a high failure than a low success

Love your neighbor, yet don't pull down your hedge.

Three may keep a secret if two of them are dead.

How can I miss you, if you won't leave?

Light Balance

DINNER

Hunters Green Salad – turkey, broccoli, mushrooms, sliced tomato, etc. on a bed of greens with *Light Balance* lemon pesto dressing served on the side. Approximately 375 calories 6.95

Chicken Florentine – 6 oz. boneless breast poached over fresh spinach and finished with lemon, served with steamed vegetables and rice. Approximately 370 calories 12.50

Chicken Lemon Pesto – 6 oz. boneless breast, grilled and glazed with lemon pesto, served with a variety of steamed vegetables & rice. Approximately 375 calories . 12.75

Broiled Filet of Sole – fresh 6 oz. portion glazed with lemon pesto, served with a variety of steamed vegetables and rice with garnish of lemon. Approximately 325 calories 13.75

Pasta Primavera – light portion of pasta du jour with julienne vegetables in a light cheese sauce. Approximately 380 calories 10.95

Light Balance
These items have been reviewed by Greenwich Nutritional Counseling Associates and are prepared with consideration given to calories, sodium & cholesterol.

SALADS

House Salad – gorgonzola or bleu 2.95

Spinach Salad – fresh spinach served with crisp bacon, sliced egg, fresh mushrooms & tomatoes. Hot dressing on request 6.95

Chef's Salad – a large bowl of mixed greens, two cheeses, ham, turkey, sliced egg, tomato & more ... a meal 7.75

Cobb Salad – shredded crisp romaine and iceberg lettuce topped with rows of diced chicken, tomato, bacon, egg, bleu cheese and avocado 7.95

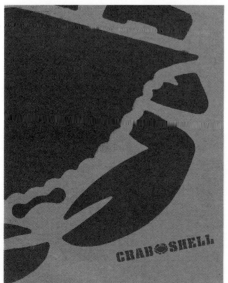

Crabshell

ADDRESS: Stamford, New York, USA

CHEF: Terence Considine

STYLE OF FOOD: Seafood

NO. OF SEATS: 136 inside, 70–120 outside

DESIGNER (Graphics): Crabshell Design, Stamford, New York, USA

DATE OF COMPLETION: 1990

GRAPHIC ELEMENTS: Menu, T-shirts, takeaway bags

Crabs, crabs and parts of crabs, rendered like a packing case or a fishing boat graphic characterize this project.

Timothy's

ADDRESS: Louisville, Kentucky, USA

CHEF: James Aydlett

STYLE OF FOOD: American Continental

NO. OF SEATS: 120

DESIGNER (Interior): Don Allen

DESIGNER (Graphics): Walter McCord, Louisville, Kentucky, USA

DATE OF COMPLETION: 1988

GRAPHIC ELEMENTS: Logo, menu, signage, small ads

I love this project for its totally unexpected (and unexplained) illustrations.

Restaurant Picasso

ADDRESS: Edwards, Colorado, USA

CHEF: Phillippe van Capellen

STYLE OF FOOD: Continental

NO. OF SEATS: 80

DESIGNER (Interior): Leon Lambotte/
Communication Arts Incorporated, Boulder,
Colorado, USA

DESIGNER (Graphics): Richard Foy, Jeni Harms
Communcation Arts Incorporated, Boulder,
Colorado, USA

DATE OF COMPLETION: 1989

GRAPHIC ELEMENTS: Logo, menu, wine list, napkins,
matchboxes and signage

No right angles about this identity, with its 'wavy'
edges and pill-popping mascot. Each menu was
handpainted and individually covered, and in the
words of the designer, 'combines European
elegance with Rocky Mountain splendour'.

Lilly's

ADDRESS: Louisville, Kentucky, USA

CHEF: Executive chef: Katherine Cary; chef: Giullia Isetti

STYLE OF FOOD: French American

NO. OF SEATS: 92

DESIGNER (Interior): Will Cary

DESIGNER (Graphics): Walter McCord, Louisville, Kentucky, USA

DATE OF COMPLETION: 1988

GRAPHIC ELEMENTS: Logo, menus, matchbooks, stationery

La General de Tetuan

ADDRESS: Barcelona, Spain

CHEF: Lorenzo Garcia Gil

STYLE OF FOOD: Spanish

NO. OF SEATS: 72

DESIGNER (Interior): Rafael del Castillo Design

DESIGNER (Graphics): Hernando Asociados, Barcelona, Spain

DATE OF COMPLETION: February 1991

GRAPHIC ELEMENTS: Menu, tablecloths, bags, matchboxes, postcards, restaurant cards, launch invitations, wrapping paper, table decorations

This wonderful lettering reminds me of old French grocery shops – or maybe old Spanish charcuteria?

PZA. TETUAN, 27
BARCELONA 08010
RESTAURANTE

La General De Tetuán

CHARCUTERIA
TEL. 265 44 77
FAX 265 77 33

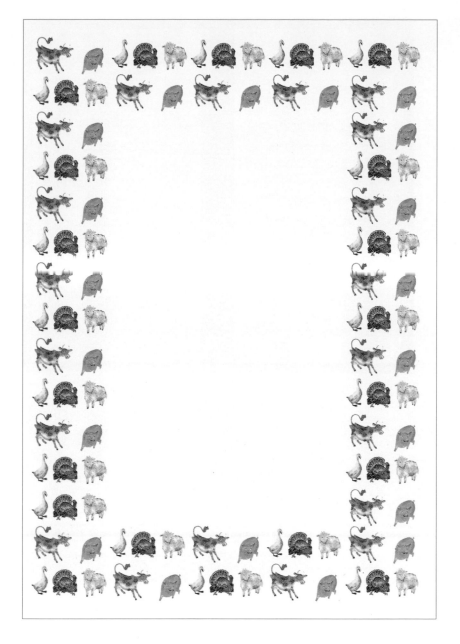

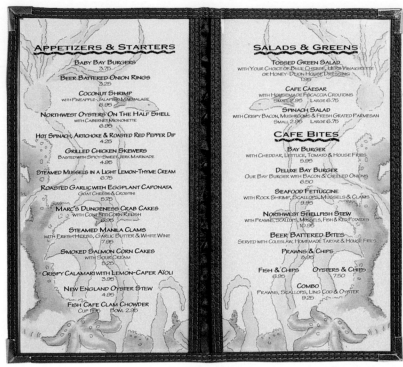

APPETIZERS & STARTERS

BABY BAY BURGERS
3.75

BEER BATTERED ONION RINGS
3.25

COCONUT SHRIMP
with Pineapple-Jalapeño Marmalade
6.95

NORTHWEST OYSTERS ON THE HALF SHELL
with Cabernet Mignonette
6.95

HOT SPINACH, ARTICHOKE & ROASTED RED PEPPER DIP
4.25

GRILLED CHICKEN SKEWERS
Basted with Spicy-Sweet Jerk Marinade
4.85

STEAMED MUSSELS IN A LIGHT LEMON-THYME CREAM
6.75

ROASTED GARLIC WITH EGGPLANT CAPONATA
Goat Cheese & Crostini
5.75

MARC'S DUNGENESS CRAB CAKES
with Confetti Corn Relish
6.95

STEAMED MANILA CLAMS
with Fresh Herbs, Garlic Butter & White Wine
7.95

SMOKED SALMON CORN CAKES
with Sour Cream
5.25

CRISPY CALAMARI WITH LEMON-CAPER AÏOLI
3.95

NEW ENGLAND OYSTER STEW
4.95

FISH CAFE CLAM CHOWDER
Cup 1.95 Bowl 2.95

SALADS & GREENS

TOSSED GREEN SALAD
with Your Choice of Blue Cheese, Herb Vinaigrette
or Honey-Dijon House Dressing
1.95

CAFE CAESAR
with Homemade Focaccia Croutons
Small 2.95 Large 6.75

SPINACH SALAD
with Crispy Bacon, Mushrooms & Fresh Grated Parmesan
Small 2.95 Large 6.75

CAFE BITES

BAY BURGER
with Cheddar, Lettuce, Tomato & House Fries
5.95

DELUXE BAY BURGER
Our Bay Burger with Bacon & Grilled Onions
6.50

SEAFOOD FETTUCCINE
with Rock Shrimp, Scallops, Mussels & Clams
9.95

NORTHWEST SHELLFISH STEW
with Prawns, Scallops, Mussels, Fish & Red Potatoes
10.95

BEER BATTERED BITES
Served with Coleslaw, Homemade Tartar & House Fries

PRAWNS & CHIPS
8.95

FISH & CHIPS   OYSTERS & CHIPS
6.95   7.50

COMBO
Prawns, Scallops, Ling Cod & Oyster
9.25

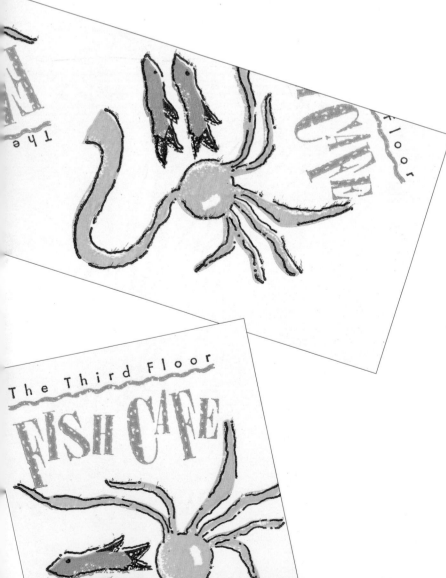

The Third Floor Fish Cafe

ADDRESS: Kirkland, Washington, USA

CHEF: Patsy Wyman/Kathy Casey

STYLE OF FOOD: Northwest seafood

NO. OF SEATS: 200

DESIGNER (Interior): Kathy Casey Inc, restaurant
Space Design

DESIGNER (Graphics): The Menu Workshop

DATE OF COMPLETION: April 1991

GRAPHIC ELEMENTS: Menus, signage, Oxford, shirts,
polo shirts, plate liners

I like the charming, whimsical drawings that
extend across every piece of literature.

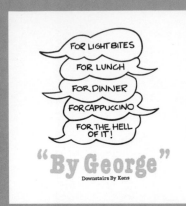

DINNER

"By George"
Downstairs By Kens

By George

ADDRESS: Boston, Massachusetts, USA

CHEF: Various

STYLE OF FOOD: New York deli

NO. OF SEATS: 200–250

DESIGNER (Interior): Howie Green Design, Boston, Massachusetts, USA

DESIGNER (Graphics): Howie Green Design, Boston, Massachusetts, USA

DATE OF COMPLETION: 1983

GRAPHIC ELEMENTS: Menus, matchboxes, coasters, napkins, T-shirts, baseball caps, aprons, placemats, advertisements

A refreshingly unconventional treatment for a restaurant

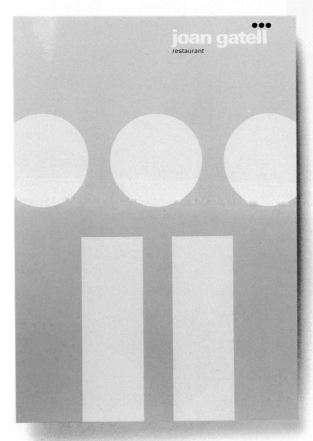

Joan Gatell

ADDRESS: Tarragona, Spain

CHEF: Joan Pedrell

STYLE OF FOOD: Seafood

NO. OF SEATS: 86

DESIGNER (Interior): Esteve Agullo and Mariano Pi/Quod, Barcelona, Spain

DESIGNER (Graphics): Josep Ma Trias/Quod, Barcelona, Spain

DATE OF COMPLETION: 1989

GRAPHIC ELEMENTS: Menu, matchboxes, ashtray

These graphics look more like corporate literature or an annual report than a restaurant, but the use of colour and shape gives an architectural feel.

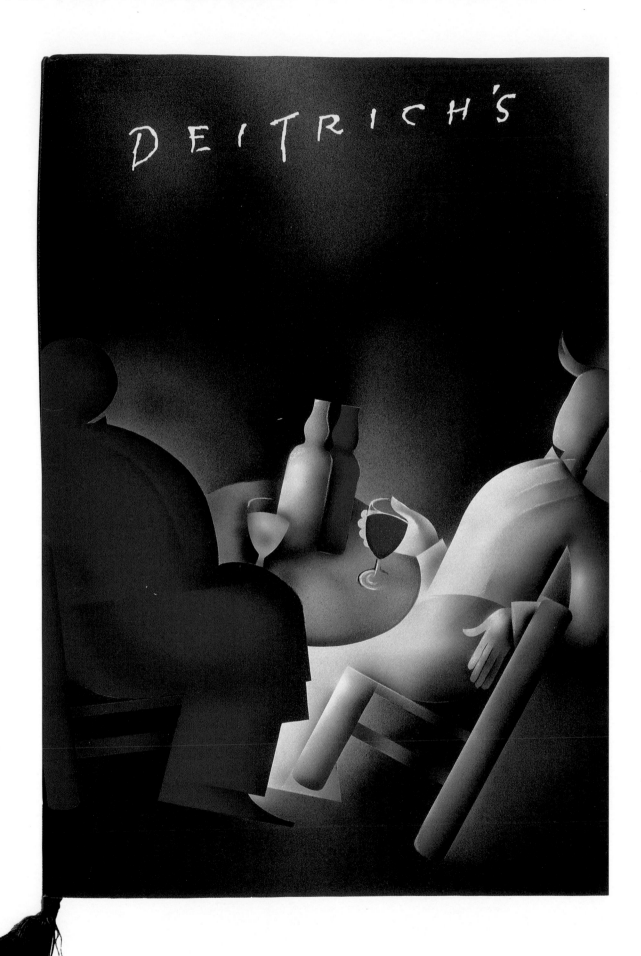

Dietrich's

ADDRESS: Louisville, Kentucky, USA
CHEF: Chip McPherson and Jeff McCracken
STYLE OF FOOD: Continental
NO. OF SEATS: 185
DESIGNER (Interior): Gianpaolo Bianconcini
DESIGNER (Graphics): Walter McCord, Louisville, Kentucky, USA
DATE OF COMPLETION: 1988
GRAPHIC ELEMENTS: Logo, signage, menus

A wonderful use of colour and airbrush illustration that undercuts its 1930s heritage with a totally modern logotype.

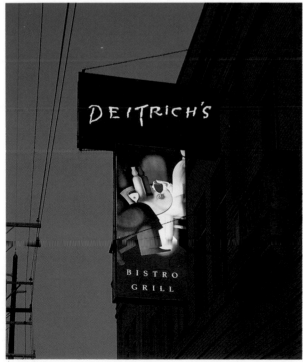

TIGER ALLEY

LUNCH

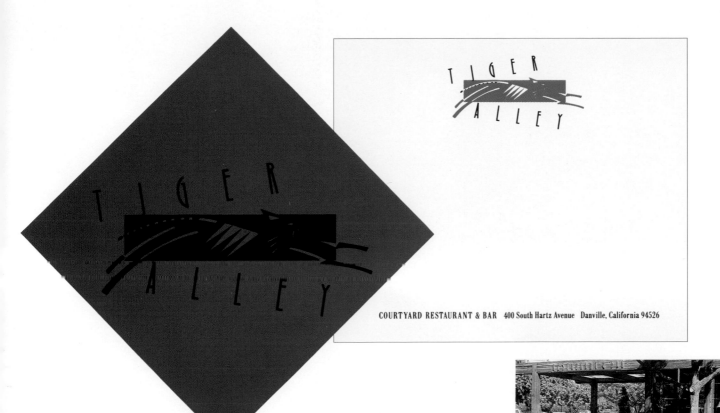

COURTYARD RESTAURANT & BAR 400 South Hartz Avenue Danville, California 94526

Tiger Alley

ADDRESS: Danville, California, USA

CHEF: James Moore

STYLE OF FOOD: Classic American

NO. OF SEATS: 150

DESIGNER (Interior): Dianne da Silva

DESIGNER (Graphics): Gerald Reis & Company, San Francisco, California, USA

DATE OF COMPLETION: 1989

GRAPHIC ELEMENTS: Signage, menus, wine list, matches, T-shirts, wine labels, water labels, stationery, press kit folder

The interior of this restaurant is somewhat formal and relies on the graphics to relieve its seriousness and associate it with its more jolly name..

Whether you like hot and spicy promotions or prefer a more delicate touch, we're offering a menu promotion that's sure to suit your taste.

From optional REAL cheese and wine selections to custom-printed menu shells, we'll supply everything you need to savor sales success.

Do you want to try our house special and reserve a promotional kit today. Simply choose from this delightful array of menu shells for a promotion made to order just for you. ◆◆◆◆◆

Midland United Dairy Industry Association

ADDRESS: Ankeny, Iowa, USA

These 'Made to Order' menus are an exercise in cross merchandising. Wine and real cheese are featured and restaurant operators choose which menu shell they want to use.

DESIGNER (Graphics): John Sayles/Sayles Graphic Design, Des Moines, Iowa, USA

DATE OF COMPLETION: 1990

GRAPHIC ELEMENTS: Matchboxes, menus, plates, napkins, T-shirts, ashtrays

These menus appear to have been inspired by the famous French advertisements for Dubonnet by A. M. Cassandre and the posters of the 1930s.

SERVICE IS
NOT INCLUDED

ALASTAIR LITTLE
RESTAURANT & BAR
49 FRITH STREET
LONDON W1V 5TE
TEL: 071-734 5183
VAT NO. 420 4416 00

09001

Alastair Little

ADDRESS: London, England

CHEF: Alastair Little

STYLE OF FOOD: Modern Eclectic

NO. OF SEATS: 34 upstairs; 18 downstairs

DESIGNER (Graphics): Brian Ma Siy, London,
England

DATE OF COMPLETION: Restaurant 1985; graphics
1990

GRAPHIC ELEMENTS: Menus, business cards,
letterheads, compliment slips, bills

There are two elements to this restaurant's
identity. The first is the corporate identity,
featuring a little ' a' (evoking the chef's name and
size); the second is more flexible and relaxed, a
Series of illustrations by the designer which
decorate the menus and change seasonally.

ALASTAIR LITTLE
RESTAURANT & BAR
49 FRITH STREET
LONDON W1V 5TE
TEL: 071-734 5183
VAT NO. 420 4416 00
REGISTERED OFFICE:
ALASTAIR LITTLE LTD
25 NEW CAVENDISH STREET
LONDON W1M 7RL
DIRECTORS: K T PEDERSEN
RA LITTLE M DOWNEND (SEC)
REGISTRATION NO. 184 37 51

ALASTAIR LITTLE
RESTAURANT & BAR
49 FRITH STREET
LONDON W1V 5TE
TEL: 071-734 5183

ALASTAIR LITTLE
RESTAURANT & BAR
49 FRITH STREET
LONDON W1V 5TE
TEL: 071-734 5183
VAT NO. 420 4416 00

Alastair Little continued over page

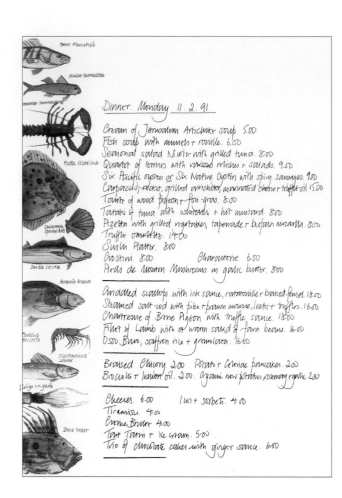

Dinner. Monday 11.2.91

Cream of Jerusalem Artichoke soup 5.00
Fish soup with mussels + rouille. 6.00
Seasonal salad Niçoise with grilled tuna. 8.00
Quartet of terrines with various relishes + salads. 9.00
Six Pacific oysters or Six Native oysters with spicy sausages. 9.00
Carpaccio, rocket, grilled artichoke, marinated cheese + truffle oil 15.00
Terrine of wood pigeon + foie-gras. 8.00
Tataki of tuna with oshitashi + hot mustard. 8.00
Pizetta with grilled vegetables, tapenade + buffalo mozarella. 8.00
Truffle omelette. 14.00
Sushi Platter. 8.00
Crostini. 8.00   Charcuterie. 6.00
Pieds de Mouton Mushrooms in garlic butter. 8.00

Griddled scallops with ink sauce, ratatouille + braised fennel. 18.00
Steamed salt-cod with pike + prawn mousse, leeks + truffles. 16.00
Chartreuse of Bone Pigeon with truffle sauce. 18.00
Fillet of Lamb with a warm salad of fava beans. 16.00
Osso Buco, saffron rice + gremolata. 16.00

Braised Chicory. 2.00   Potato + Celeriac pancakes. 2.00
Broccoli + lemon oil. 2.00   Organic new potatoes, rosemary + garlic. 2.00

Cheeses. 6.00   Ices + sorbets. 4.00
Tiramisu. 4.00
Creme Brulee 4.00
Tart Tatin + ice cream. 5.00
Trio of chocolate cakes with ginger sauce. 6.00

DINNER DOWNSTAIRS
WEDNESDAY 10.10.90

Crostini 8.00
Sashimi of Tuna 12.00
Grilled vegetable salad 6.00
Carpaccio 15.00
Charcuterie 6.00
Sushi and tuna tataki roll 8.00
Chilled Cucumber soup with raita 5.00

Tomato and bufala mozzarella salad 8.00
Six pacific oysters and shallot relish 8.00
Ratatouille and spinach charlotte 8.00
Duo of terrines 8.00
Pig's trotters baked in a mustard and herb crust 6.00
Capon tomato and plum tomato and basil salad 7.00
Soused herrings, prints and cucumber salads 6.00
Pizetta with grilled vegetables, tapenade + mozzarella 8.00
Side salad 2.50

Cheeses 6.00
Ices and sorbets 4.00
Creme brulee 4.00
Summer pudding 6.00
Hazelnut parfait with summer fruit
Mirabelle tart with creme fraiche
Tiramisu 4.00
Dark and white chocolate truffle cake and
ginger ice-cream 6.00

Alastair Little continued

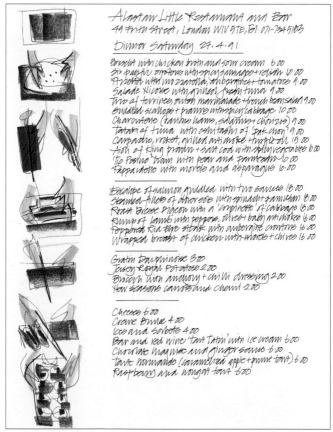

Alastair Little Restaurant and Bar
49 Frith Street, London W1V 5TE, Tel: 071-734 5183
Dinner Saturday 27.4.91

Borscht with chicken broth and sour cream 6.00
Six pacific oysters with spicy sausages + relish 10.00
Pizetta with mozzarella, anchovies + tomatoes 8.00
Salade Niçoise with grilled fresh tuna 9.00
Trio of terrines, onion marmalade + french bean salad 9.00
Griddled scallops + prawns with spicy cabbage 10.00
Charcuterie (Parma hams, salamis + chorizo) 9.00
Tataki of tuna with oshitashi + bok choy 9.00
Carpaccio, rocket, grilled artichoke + truffle oil 15.00
Fish of King prawn + salt cod with spicy vegetables 8.00
Trio Pecorino Toscano with pear and pancetta 10.00
Pappardelle with morels and asparagus 6.00

Escalope of salmon griddled with two sauces 18.00
Steamed fillets of John Dory with spinach + parmesan 18.00
Roast Bresse Pigeon with a 'vinaigrette' of cabbage 18.00
Rump of lamb with peppers, olives + baby artichoke 16.00
Peppered Rib-eye steak with aubergine crostino 16.00
Wrapped breast of chicken with morels + chives 16.00

Gratin Dauphinoise 3.00
Jersey Royal potatoes 2.00
Broccoli with anchovy + chilli dressing 2.00
New seasons carrots and chervil 2.00

Cheeses 6.00
Creme brulee 4.00
Ices and sorbets 4.00
Bar and red wine 'tart Tatin' with ice cream 6.00
Chocolate marquise and ginger sauce 6.00
Tarte normande (caramelized apple + prune tart) 6.00
Raspberry and nougat tart 6.00

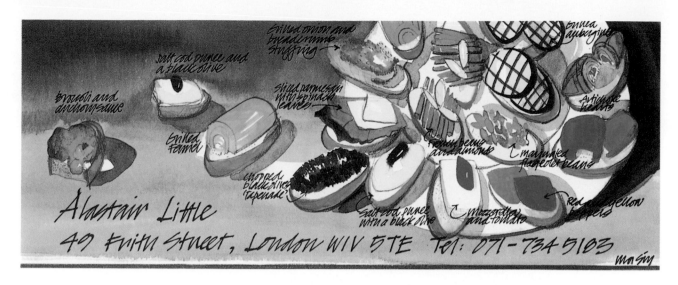

Alastair Little
49 Frith Street, London W1V 5TE Tel: 071-734 5103

DINNER DOWNSTAIRS THURSDAY 31·1·91

Chicken soup with ricotta dumplings 6·00
Sauted cockles and palourdes with cream and thyme 8·00
Seasonal salad with prawn toasts and mexican garnishes 10·00
Grilled vegetable and anchovy salad 6·00
Crostini 6·00
Charcuterie 6·00
Six pacific oysters and shallot relish 7·00
Sushi, salmon and avocado roll 8·00
Cajun salad manhuan style with plum tomatoes 8·00
Seafood salad (squid, prawns, mussels, cockles, clams) 8·00
Braised ox-tongue with beetroot and a celeriac purée 14·00
Braised breast of veal and spinach 12·00
Carpaccio 15·00
Trio of terrines 9·00
Truffle omlette with free range eggs 14·00
Organic potatoes with chives and butter 2·00
Side salad 2·50   Rocket salad 4·00

Cheeses 6·00
Ices and sorbets 4·00
Creme brulée 4·00
Tiramisu 4·00
Pear, quince and almond tart 5·00
Dark and white chocolate truffle cake and gingersauce 6·00
Creme caramel with blood orange salad 5·00

BIBENDUM

NUNC EST BIBENDUM

OYSTER BAR

Bibendum

ADDRESS: London, England

CHEF: Simon Hopkinson

STYLE OF FOOD: French country food

NO. OF SEATS: 75

DESIGNER (Interior): Sir Terence Conran

DESIGNER (Graphics): RSCG Conran Design, London, England

DATE OF COMPLETION: November 1987

GRAPHIC ELEMENTS: Menus, plates, glasses, napkins, ashtrays, postcards

Sir Terence Conran's transformation of one of London's most beautiful art nouveau buildings draws its graphic inspiration from the decorative elements of the one-time Michelin tyre depot and the famous Michelin man, set in mosaic in the forecourt.

Etrusca

ADDRESS: San Francisco, California, USA

CHEF: Ruggero Gadaldi

STYLE OF FOOD: Italian

NO. OF SEATS: 100

DESIGNER (Graphics): Nicholas Sidjakov and Barbara Vick/SBG Partners, San Francisco, California, USA; illustrator: Heather Preston; photographer: Karen Montgomery

DATE OF COMPLETION: 1990

GRAPHIC ELEMENTS: Menus, wine list, matchbooks, business stationery

Quarterdeck

ADDRESS: Glenelg, South Australia, Australia

CHEF: Ray Mauger

STYLE OF FOOD: Seafood and prime beef

NO. OF SEATS: 120

DESIGNER (Interior): Terry Feltus Architect

DESIGNER (Graphics): Gayle Mason Design, Wayville, South Australia, Australia

DATE OF COMPLETION: October 1990

GRAPHIC ELEMENTS: Menus, placemats

The Rusty Pelican

ADDRESS: Nationwide chain throughout the USA

CHEF: Various

STYLE OF FOOD: Seafood

NO. OF SEATS: Varies according to venue

DESIGNER (Graphics): Dean Gerrie Designs, Santa Ana, California, USA; photography Russel Sasaki

DATE OF COMPLETION: March 1990

GRAPHIC ELEMENTS: Menus, employee handbook, direct mail flyers, wine menus, exterior signage

A huge range of print in a variety of graphic styles from one venue.

Rusty Pelican continued over page

Wine

Rusty Pelican continued

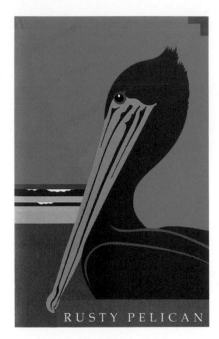

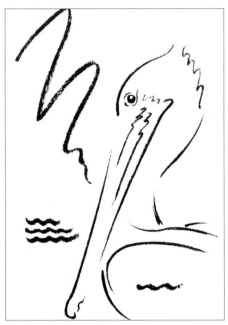

LUNCH

FRESH SALADS

SAUTEED SEAFOOD SALAD 6.95
Scallops, shrimp, fresh zucchini & bacon sauteed in white wine then poured over fresh crisp greens and sprinkled with jack cheese—Rusty's favorite

PASTA AND CHICKEN SALAD 6.25
Chunks of tender white meat chicken tossed with chilled shell pasta, garden fresh vegetables, provolone cheese, and Italian dressing.

PASTA AND SHRIMP SALAD 7.25
Chilled shell pasta, bay shrimp, fresh broccoli, zucchini, carrots, bell pepper and tomatoes all mixed with Italian dressing and provolone cheese.

FRESH SPINACH SALAD 5.25
Avocado, chopped egg, real bacon—and more!

CHILLED SEAFOOD LOUIES
with Crab 7.95 with shrimp 6.95

MAC'S LUNCH 4.95
A bowl of Rusty's clam chowder and a tossed green or fresh spinach salad with choice of dressings: Homemade blue cheese, red raspberry vinaigrette or chilled Italian bacon.

ENTREES
Entrees are served with freshly baked San Francisco sourdough bread, freshly made coleslaw and your choice of French fries, fresh sliced tomatoes or pasta salad.

FRESH CLAM FETTUCCINE 7.45
Tender diced clams in our creamy Alfredo sauce over fettuccine pasta with fresh parmesan cheese...topped with fresh steamed clams.

COQUILLE ST. PELICAN 7.25
Scallops, shrimp & crab smothered in creamed mushroom sauce—melted cheese atop.

CALAMARI STEAK 6.25
Tender calamari (squid) steak lightly breaded and sauteed to a golden brown.

CASHEW SHRIMP 8.25
Tender whole shrimp stir fried with fresh snow pea pods, broccoli, onions, red peppers, mushrooms, sprouts and a special oriental sauce.

CROISSANT SANDWICHES
(We bake our own.)

BAY SHRIMP & AVOCADO 6.25
With sliced cucumber & 1000 island dressing—on a fresh croissant.

CLUB CROISSANT 5.95
Sliced turkey breast, Swiss cheese and bacon with fresh sliced cucumber.

ROAST BEEF & MUENSTER CHEESE 5.50
Thin sliced cold roast beef, cheese & cucumber with Dijon mustard on a fresh croissant.

CHICKEN TERIYAKI 6.95
Boneless breast of chicken marinated in our own famous teriyaki sauce, broiled golden brown.

RUSTY'S HAMBURGER 5.25
Topped with melted Cheddar—served on a fresh roll.

THE LANDLUBBER 5.95
Hot roast beef, avocado and tomato covered with melted Muenster and Cheddar cheeses on sprouted 7-grain whole wheat bread.

CASHEW CHICKEN 7.25
Just like our stir-fry shrimp, but with boneless chunks of tender white meat chicken breast.

FRESH PAN-FRIED OYSTERS 5.95
Dipped in egg, lightly breaded then fried in butter to a golden brown.

Rusty's homemade chowders, fresh salads or Rusty's garlic bread 1.75

DESSERTS
We make our own desserts—using only the freshest ingredients

Chocolate Pecan Pie 3.25
(Triple Chocolate Treat)

Cheesecake 2.75   Irresistible Mud Pie 3.25

Haagen-Daz Flavor of the Day 2.75

Fresh Ground Coffee .85

Tea .85   Brewed Decaffeinated Coffee .85   Milk .85

Sales tax will be added to all food and beverage purchased in the Dining Room.

The Pier

ADDRESS: Des Moines, Iowa, USA

STYLE OF FOOD: Seafood

NO. OF SEATS: 185

DESIGNER (Graphics): John Sayles/Sayles Graphic Design, Des Moines, Iowa, USA

DATE OF COMPLETION: 1988 and ongoing

This advertising campaign was developed to promote an 11-year old seafood restaurant. The campaign included billboards, direct mail and newspaper ads.

The Fish Co.

ADDRESS: Santa Monica, California, USA

CHEF: Randy LaFerr

STYLE OF FOOD: Mesquite seafood

NO. OF SEATS: 250

DESIGNER (Interior): Susan Rogers/Rusty Kay & Associates, Santa Monica, California, USA

DESIGNER (Graphics): Susan Rogers/Rusty Kay & Associates, Santa Monica, California, USA

DATE OF COMPLETION: 1990

GRAPHIC ELEMENTS: Menu, logo

This identity was also applied to 50 buses and direct mail postcards as part of an advertising campaign designed by Keith Puccinelli, Santa Barbara, California, USA.

La Masia at Tibidabo

ADDRESS: Barcelona, Spain

CHEF: Inma Buxeres/Juan Canas

STYLE OF FOOD: International

NO. OF SEATS: 180

DESIGNER (Interior): Jordi Gali/CR Communication
& Design Services SA, Barcelona, Spain

DESIGNER (Graphics): Carlos Rolando/CR
Communication & Design Services SA, Barcelona,
Spain

DATE OF COMPLETION: June 1989

GRAPHIC ELEMENTS: Logo, menu

High quality and understatement is evoked by the
use of embossing and thick paper.

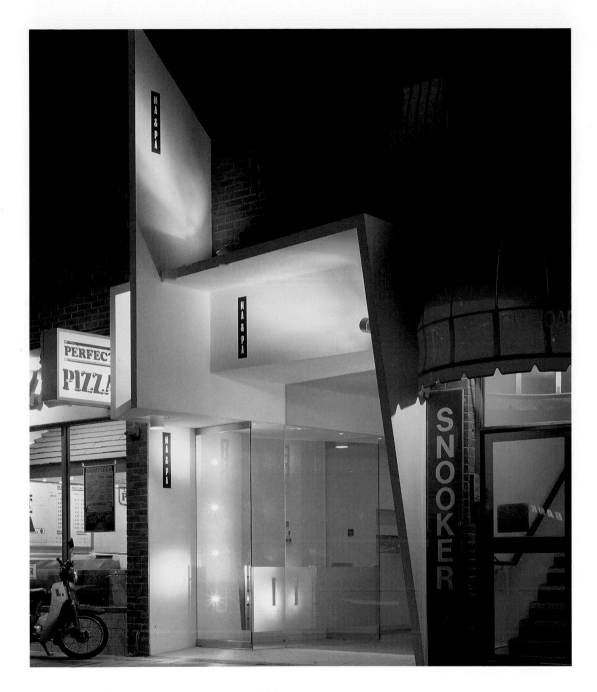

Ma & Pa

ADDRESS: London, England
NO. OF SEATS: 120
DESIGNER (Interior): Rick Mather Architects,
London, England
DESIGNER (Graphics): Rick Mather Architects,
London, England
DATE OF COMPLETION: 1989

Ma and Pa is now a Chinese restaurant and
renamed The Dragon House, but its original
exterior still stands.

CAPELLINI "Fine Hairs" very fine pasta.

PENNE "Pens" or "Feathers"; pasta tubes cut diagonally at both ends, like a quill pen, into short lengths.

DITALINI "Little Thimbles"; small macaroni, cut at very short lengths; used in minestrone soup.

RAVIOLI The well known pasta squares, stuffed with eggs, vegetables, or cheeses.

FETTUCCINE "Small Ribbons"; one of the best known Italian Pastas.

RIGATONI "Large Grooves" pasta tubes.

FUSILLI "Spindles"; Pasta twisted like corkscrews.

SPAGHETTI "Length of cord or string"; it is a word that describes the most famous product of all, a solid round rod.

GNOCCHI "Dumplings"; a pasta dumpling typically made with potatoes.

TORTELLINI "Small Twists"; little rings of dough stuffed with meats, filings are formed pork, turkey, chicken and cheeses. A real specialty.

LINGUINE "Small Tongues"; in the shape of flattened spaghetti but may range in diameter.

ZITONI A hollow or pierced pasta tube. Can be served in lengths like spaghetti but more often is cut into "bite size" pieces and served in its "ziti".

MARUZZELLE "Small Seashells"; typically used in salad pasta salads.

Italian and French
Restaurants This selection of work shows

how widespread the influence of Italian and French

cuisine has now become. Many of the best design

solutions in this area come from the USA.

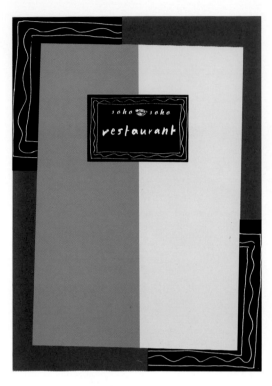

Soho Soho

ADDRESS: London, England

CHEF: Donny Howorth

STYLE OF FOOD: French Provençal

NO. OF SEATS: 175

DESIGNER (Interior): Virgile & Stone Associates Ltd, London, England

DESIGNER (Graphics): Virgile & Stone Associates Ltd, London, England

DATE OF COMPLETION: October 1991

GRAPHIC ELEMENTS: Menus, wine list, business card, murals, stationery, matches

Both the interior and the graphics have been done by the same team of designers so the elements which reflect the South of France, the theme of this venue, are shared by both. The bright sunny hues of the menus, the quality of the lighting, the dual colours of the upholstery and the bold Matisse-style murals (by Jan Turner) all play their part.

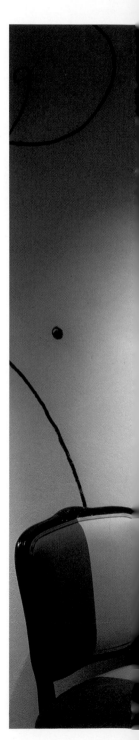

Giorgio's Cafe

ADDRESS: New York City, New York, USA

CHEF: Keith Seidner

STYLE OF FOOD: Italian Metro

NO. OF SEATS: 90 plus delivery area

DESIGNER (Interior): Gene L. Nemeth

DESIGNER (Graphics): Fenton F. Engl, King F. Lai, The Marketing Partnership, New York City, New York, USA

DATE OF COMPLETION: February 1989

GRAPHIC ELEMENTS: Exterior facade, signage, stationery, menu, napkins, place settings, matchboxes, delivery packaging (menu, box and microwavable custom plate with cover), corporate accounts kit

A curiously memorable typographic solution, which accentuates the 'Gio' part of the name, is implemented across dozens of items.

Giorgio continued over page

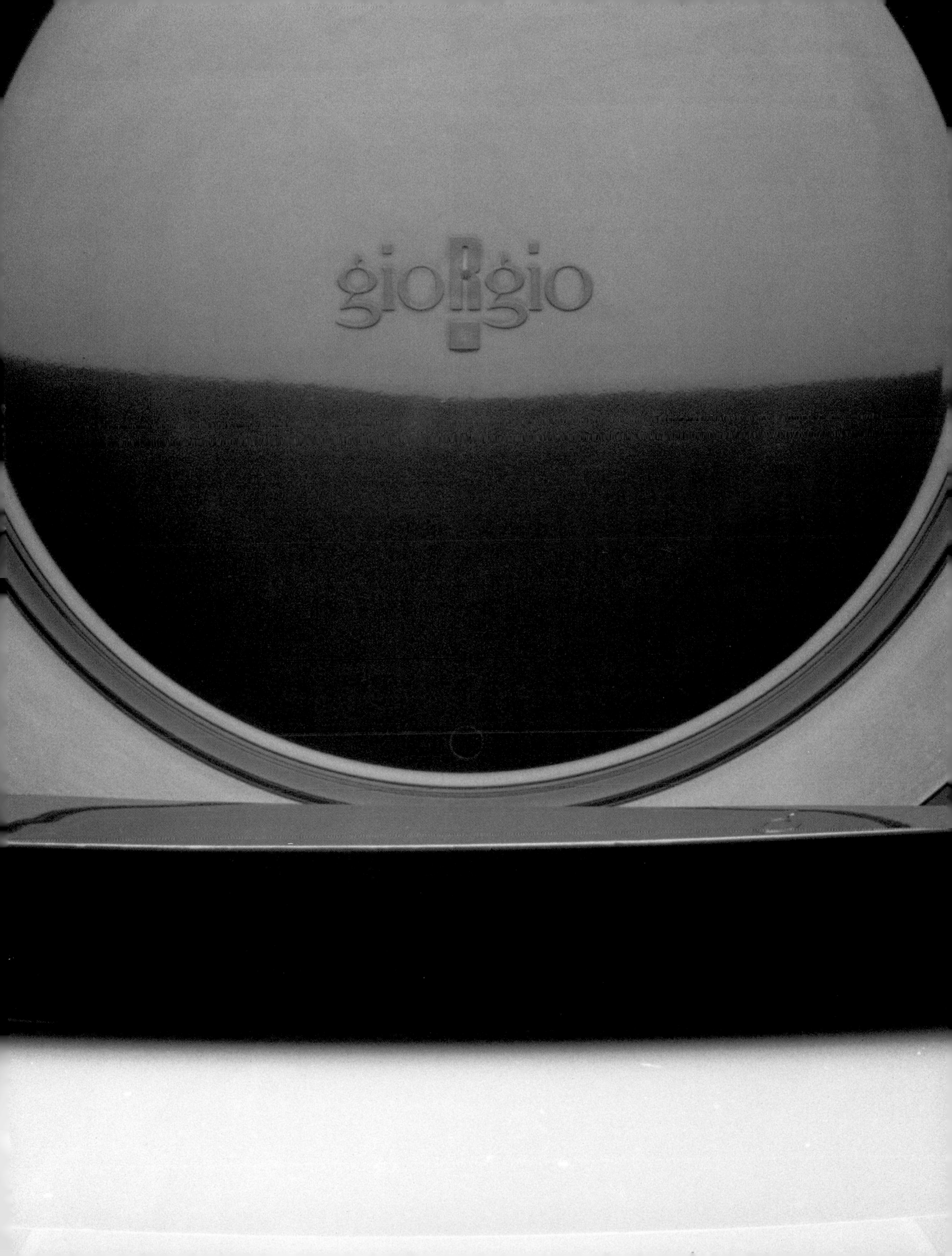
giorgio

Giorgio continued

GIORGIO CAFE   245 PARK AVENUE SOUTH
NEW YORK, NEW YORK 10003

GIORGIO CAFE   245 PARK AVENUE SOUTH
NEW YORK, NEW YORK 10003 (212)460-5858
FAX: (212)460-5086

GIORGIO CAFE 245 PARK AVENUE SOUTH
NEW YORK, NEW YORK 10003 (212)460-5858
FAX: (212)460-5086 DELIVERY: (212)460-9100

Zia's Cucina Genuina

ADDRESS: Sugarland, Texas, USA

CHEF: No chef: family recipes

STYLE OF FOOD: Northern and Southern Italian food

NO. OF SEATS: 160

DESIGNER (Interior): Architect: Jack Rimes; interior designer: Yvonne Heizer

DESIGNER (Graphics): The Bradford Lawton Design Group, San Antonio, Texas, USA

DATE OF COMPLETION: 1988

GRAPHIC ELEMENTS: Logos, menus

This logo seems to spring freshly rolled off the pasta tray and I like the feeling of choice and expertise about the background patterns. Even the paper inside the menu evokes pasta dough.

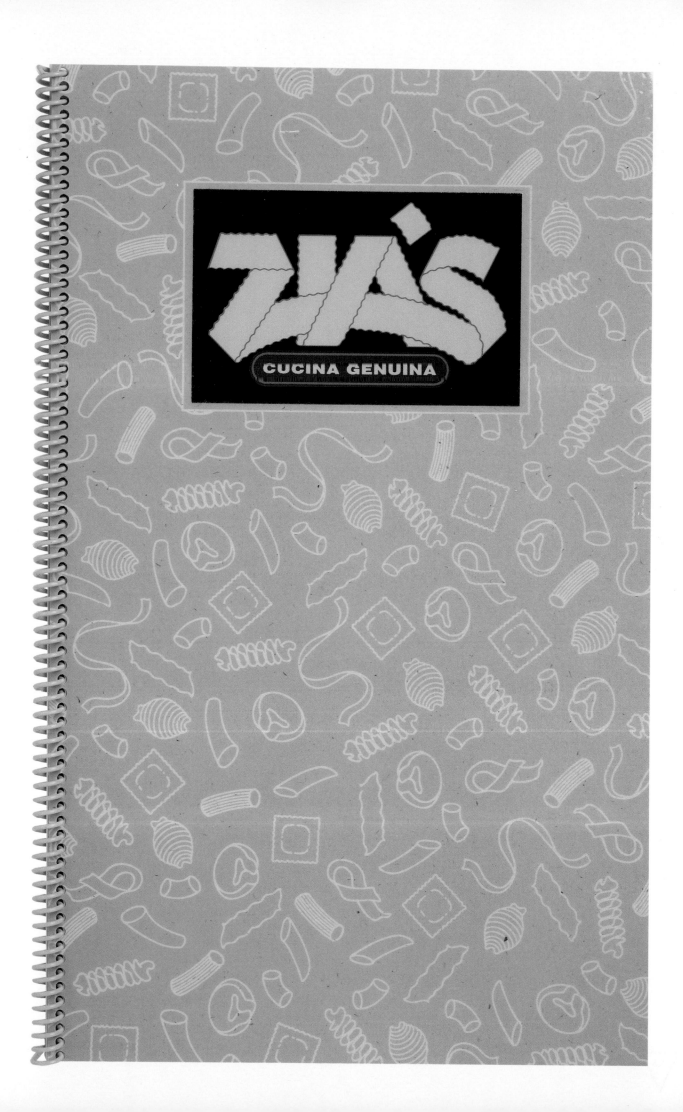

SISLEY
ITALIAN KITCHEN

Sisley Italian Kitchen

ADDRESS: Los Angeles, California, USA

CHEF: Steve Noschese

STYLE OF FOOD: Italian Californian Cuisine

NO. OF SEATS: 130

DESIGNER (Interior): Saeed Hedjazi Architects,
Los Angeles, California, USA

DESIGNER (Graphics): Greg Clarke, Vickie Sawyer
Karten/Josh Freeman Associates, Los Angeles,
California, USA

DATE OF COMPLETION: April 1990

GRAPHIC ELEMENTS: Menu, apron, business cards,
T-shirts, signage

The logo and application of the graphics
successfully avoid all the usual Italian clichés and it
looks fresh and timeless.

Oli-Ola Trattoria Toscana

ADDRESS: Pacific Palisades, California, USA

CHEF: Augustino Sciandra

STYLE OF FOOD: Northern Italian

NO. OF SEATS: 50

DESIGNER (Interior): Kathleen Gordon

DESIGNER (Graphics): Kim Baer Design; signage by
Stuart Karten Design, Marina Del Rey,
California, USA

DATE OF COMPLETION: March 1991

GRAPHIC ELEMENTS: Menu, letterhead, business
cards, envelopes, matches, signage

15200 Sunset Boulevard
(enter on La Cruz)
Pacific Palisades, CA
90272

•

213.459.9214

Olí·Olá • Killer Deal Enterprises, Inc.
Restaurant • 15200 Sunset Boulevard, Pacific Palisades, California 90272 • 213.459.9214
Business Office • 11812 San Vicente Boulevard, Suite 200, Los Angeles, California 90049

15200 Sunset Boulevard, Pacific Palisades, California 90272

13200 Sunset Boulevard ■ Pacific Palisades 90272

Photo by Bruce Rothfield

Red Tomato

ADDRESS: Chicago, Illinois, USA

CHEF: Ed Reeba/Joe Divinere

STYLE OF FOOD: Italian

NO. OF SEATS: 80

DESIGNER (Interior): Keith Youngquist,
Aumiller Youngquist PC/Mount Prospect, Illinois,
USA

DESIGNER (Graphics): Joed Design, Chicago, Illinois,
USA

DATE OF COMPLETION: June 1990

GRAPHIC ELEMENTS: Logo, menus, stationery

A curious mixture of styles – hand-drawn
'supermarket' with airbrushed 1930s and natural
textures. The result doesn't look at all Italian – but
why should it?

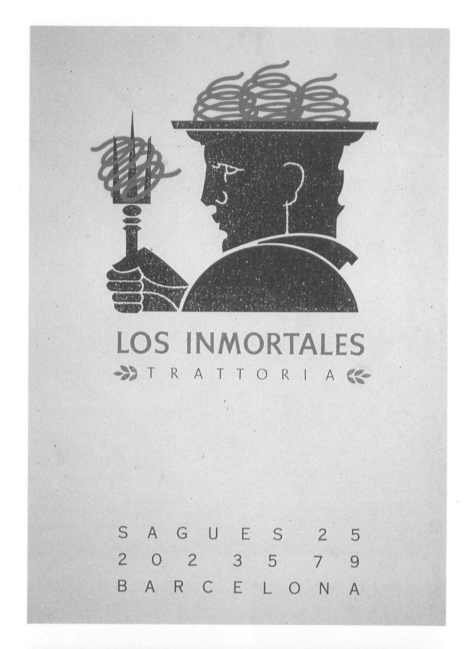

Los Inmortales

ADDRESS: Chain of two restaurants in Barcelona, Spain

CHEF: Flavio Ori (first restaurant): Juan Carlos Vega (second restaurant)

STYLE OF FOOD: Italian

NO. OF SEATS: 75 (first restaurant); 45 (second restaurant)

DESIGNER (Interior): Enrique Granell & Marc Cuixart

DESIGNER (Graphics): Carlos Rolando/CR Communications Barcelona, Spain

DATE OF COMPLETION: April 1980 (second restaurant); June 1988 (first restaurant)

GRAPHIC ELEMENTS: Logos, menu cards, murals based on Etruscan murals

I like this witty adaptation of an illustration by Robert Foster for a 1928 American magazine cover.

Spuntino

ADDRESS: San Francisco, California, USA

CHEF: Karen Fullerton

STYLE OF FOOD: Italian fast food

NO. OF SEATS: 90 plus counter seats

DESIGNER (Interior):

DESIGNER (Graphics): Rod Dyer Group, Los Angeles, California, USA

DATE OF COMPLETION: 1990

GRAPHIC ELEMENTS: Menu

The logo for this menu is colourful and fun, a nice relaxed use of type that gives no hint of the style of interior or the cuisine available there.

Mama Ilardo's

ADDRESS: Baltimore, Maryland and Washington
DC, USA

CHEF: Various

STYLE OF FOOD: Pizza, pasta, speciality Italian
dishes

NO. OF SEATS: Chain of restaurants: seating varies

DESIGNER (Graphics): W. Scott Mahr, The Menu
Design Group, New York City, New York, USA

DATE OF COMPLETION: October 1988

GRAPHIC ELEMENTS: Signage, menus, interior
murals

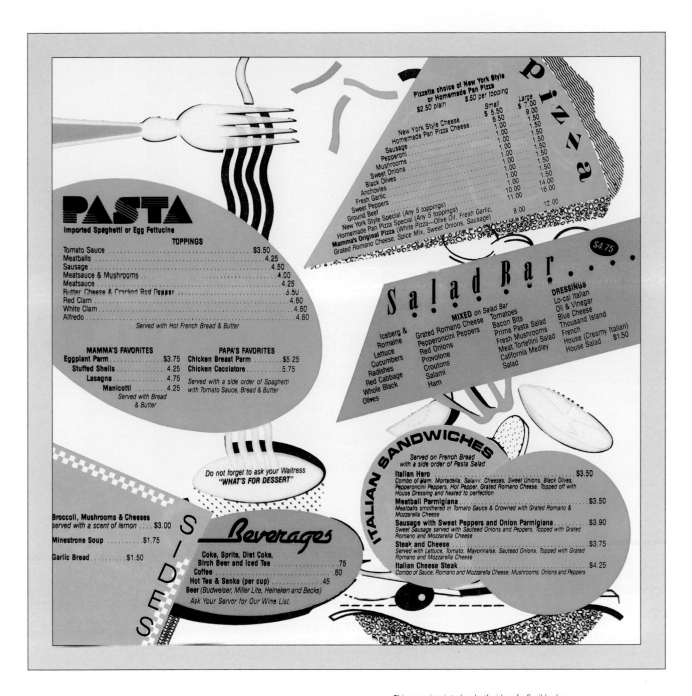

PASTA
Imported Spaghetti or Egg Fettucine

TOPPINGS

Tomato Sauce	$3.50
Meatballs	4.25
Sausage	4.50
Meatsauce & Mushrooms	4.00
Meatsauce	4.25
Butter, Cheese & Cracked Red Pepper	3.50
Red Clam	4.60
White Clam	4.60
Alfredo	4.60

Served with Hot French Bread & Butter

MAMMA'S FAVORITES
Eggplant Parm	$3.75
Stuffed Shells	4.25
Lasagna	4.75
Manicotti	4.25

Served with Bread & Butter

PAPA'S FAVORITES
Chicken Breast Parm	$5.25
Chicken Cacciatore	5.75

Served with a side order of Spaghetti with Tomato Sauce, Bread & Butter

Pizza

Pizzetta choice of New York Style or Homemade Pan Pizza
$2.50 plain $.50 per topping

	Small	Large
	$ 5.50	$ 7.00
New York Style Cheese	5.50	9.00
Homemade Pan Pizza Cheese	6.50	
	1.00	1.50
Sausage	1.00	1.50
Pepperoni	1.00	1.50
Mushrooms	1.00	1.50
Sweet Onions	1.00	1.50
Black Olives	1.00	1.50
Anchovies	1.00	1.50
Fresh Garlic	10.00	14.00
Sweet Peppers	10.00	16.00
Ground Beef	11.00	
New York Style Special (Any 5 toppings)		
Homemade Pan Pizza Special (Any 5 toppings)	8.00	12.00

Mamma's Original Pizza (White Pizza—Olive Oil, Fresh Garlic, Grated Romano Cheese, Spice Mix, Sweet Onions, Sausage)

Salad Bar.... $4.75

MIXED on Salad Bar
Iceberg & Romaine Lettuce
Cucumbers
Radishes
Red Cabbage
Whole Black Olives

Grated Romano Cheese
Pepperoncini Peppers
Red Onions
Provolone
Croutons
Salami
Ham

Tomatoes
Bacon Bits
Prima Pasta Salad
Fresh Mushrooms
Meat Tortellini Salad
California Medley
Salad

DRESSINGS
Lo-cal Italian
Oil & Vinegar
Blue Cheese
Thousand Island
French
House (Creamy Italian)
House Salad .. $1.50

ITALIAN SANDWICHES
Served on French Bread with a side order of Pasta Salad

Italian Hero	$3.50

Combo of Ham, Mortadella, Salami, Cheeses, Sweet Onions, Black Olives, Pepperoncini Peppers, Hot Pepper, Grated Romano Cheese, Topped off with House Dressing and heated to perfection

Meatball Parmigiana	$3.50

Meatballs smothered in Tomato Sauce & Crowned with Grated Romano & Mozzarella Cheese

Sausage with Sweet Peppers and Onion Parmigiana	$3.90

Sweet Sausage served with Sauteed Onions and Peppers, Topped with Grated Romano and Mozzarella Cheese

Steak and Cheese	$3.75

Served with Lettuce, Tomato, Mayonnaise, Sauteed Onions, Topped with Grated Romano and Mozzarella Cheese

Italian Cheese Steak	$4.25

Combo of Sauce, Romano and Mozzarella Cheese, Mushrooms, Onions and Peppers

SIDES

Broccoli, Mushrooms & Cheeses served with a scent of lemon	$3.00
Minestrone Soup	$1.75
Garlic Bread	$1.50

Do not forget to ask your Waitress "WHAT'S FOR DESSERT"

Beverages

Coke, Sprite, Diet Coke, Birch Beer and Iced Tea	.75
Coffee	.60
Hot Tea & Sanka (per cup)	.45

Beer (Budweiser, Miller Lite, Heineken and Becks)

Ask Your Server for Our Wine List.

This menu is printed on both sides of a flexible clear acetate; I wonder what Mama would have thought, if she were alive now!

Esprit de Provence

THE PORTMAN GRILL

Esprit de Provence

ADDRESS : San Francisco, California, USA

CHEF : Fred Halpert

STYLE OF FOOD : Southern French cuisine

DESIGNER (Graphics): Elizabeth Berta/

Jody Thompson, The Thompson Design Group,

San Francisco, California, USA

DATE OF COMPLETION : April 1989

GRAPHIC ELEMENTS : Menus, opening invitation

Sud-Ouest

ADDRESS: London, England

CHEF: David Shuttleworth

STYLE OF FOOD: Provencal (French)

NO. OF SEATS: 100; plus 70 in cafe

DESIGNER (Interior): Guy Willis and Louise Pont, Bosworth Field, London, England

DESIGNER (Graphics): Anthony Warren and Oliver Wheeler, Bosworth Field, London, England

DATE OF COMPLETION: November 1989

GRAPHIC ELEMENTS: Menus, winelists, matchbooks, postcards, stationery, receipts, bills, internal and external signage, screen printed window signs

Good consistent application and nice use of an evocative hand-drawn letterform which looks both contemporary and ethnic at the same time.

Sud-Ouest continued over page

Sud-Ouest continued

Sud-Ouest continued

27-31 Basil Street, London SW3 1BB
Tel:071-584 4484 Fax:071-584 7291 Accounts:071-584 9099

27-31 Basil Street, London SW3 1BB
Tel:071-584 4484 Fax:071-584 7291 Accounts:071-584 9099

With Compliments

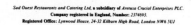

Sud Ouest Restaurants and Catering Ltd, a subsidiary of Aretusa Crucial Enterprises PLC.
Company registered in England, Number: 2374693.
Registered Office: Lynwood House, 24-32 Kilburn High Road, London NW6 5UJ

27-31 Basil Street, London SW3 1BB
Tel:071-584 4484 Fax: 071-584 7291 Accounts:071-584 9099

Regional and Ethnic Restaurants

Design solutions in this category often need to be more specific if they intend to convey the style of the food or the ingredient. But as the range of regional food becomes more varied, often mixing two or three themes together — Spanish and Mexican, Californian and Oriental (known as Pacific Rim), Cajun and Creole (Delta) — so the design options are also opened up.

Nine Spice

ADDRESS: London, England

CHEF: Various

STYLE OF FOOD: Indian

NO. OF SEATS: 40 (average)

DESIGNER (Interior): Godsmark Gordon, London,
England

DESIGNER (Graphics): Godsmark Gordon/Bostock &
Pollitt, London, England

DATE OF COMPLETION: 1989

GRAPHIC ELEMENTS: Logo, menus, napkins,
matchboxes

How nice to see an Indian restaurant without any
of the usual trappings of ethnic symbolism.
The only visual reference to the subcontinent is the
stylized saffron turban.

China Joe

ADDRESS: London, England

CHEF: Various

STYLE OF FOOD: Chinese diner and takeaway

DESIGNER (Interior): Godsmark Gordon, London, England

DESIGNER (Graphics): Godsmark Gordon, London, England/Bostock & Pollitt, London, England

DATE OF COMPLETION: December 1987

GRAPHIC ELEMENTS: Logo, menus, china, stationery

Very much a 1980s 'painterly' solution – fresh, nicely executed and right for its market.

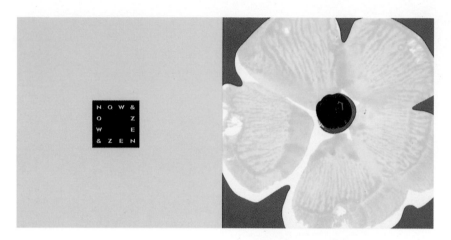

ZEN Restaurants

ADDRESS: London, England

EXECUTIVE CHEF: Michael Leung

CHEFS: Wing Fong Wong (NOW & ZEN); Shui Lin Wong (ZEN Chelsea); Kowk Lee Tang (ZENW3); Cho Kai Lo (ZEN Mayfair)

STYLE OF FOOD: Chinese

NO. OF SEATS: 170/200 (NOW & ZEN); 120 (ZEN Chelsea); 150 (ZENW3); 90 (ZEN Mayfair)

DESIGNER (Interior): Rick Mather Architects, London, England

DESIGNER (Graphics): Rick Mather Architects, London, England

DATE OF COMPLETION: NOW & ZEN: 1991; ZEN Mayfair: 1987; ZENW3: 1986

GRAPHIC ELEMENTS: Menus, chopstick packs, toothpick packs, matchbooks, chocolate wrappers, napkins, placemats

This chain of restaurants features clever adaptations of the zen symbol, a masterly evocation of calm and simplicity. Howard Waller designed all the graphics and promotion material using a series of poppy paintings by Peter Denmark. Some guests came to the restaurant opening solely because of the design of the invitation: praise indeed.

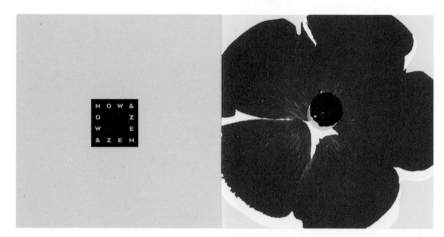

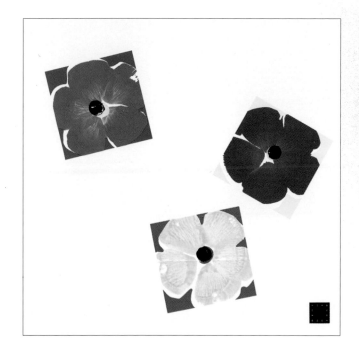

ZEN restaurants continued over page

ZEN restaurants continued

NOW & ZEN, London, England (above)

ZEN W3, London, England (right)

China Grill

ADDRESS: New York City, New York, USA

CHEF: Peter Klein

STYLE OF FOOD: California/French with oriental
influence

NO. OF SEATS: 230

DESIGNER (Interior): Jeffrey G. Beers Architects,
New York City, New York, USA

DESIGNER (Graphics): Tibor Kalman and David
Riccardi/M & Co, New York City, New York, USA

DATE OF COMPLETION: 1987

GRAPHIC ELEMENTS: Menu, matchboxes, business
cards, plates, T-shirts

The French/Oriental influence in the menu is
represented in both the graphics and the
interior by the use of passages from the
Journals of Marco Polo, chronicling his travels
in China.

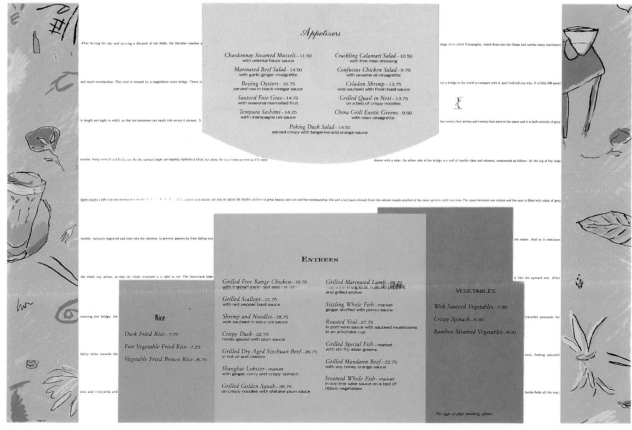

Appetizers

Chardonnay Steamed Mussels—11.50
with oriental flavor sauce

Crackling Calamari Salad—10.50
with lime miso dressing

Marinated Beef Salad—14.50
with garlic ginger vinaigrette

Confucius Chicken Salad—9.75
with sesame oil vinaigrette

Beijing Oysters—10.75
served raw in black vinegar sauce

Celadon Shrimp—13.75
wok sauteed with fresh basil sauce

Sauteed Foie Gras—14.75
with seasonal marinated fruit

Grilled Quail in Nest—13.75
on a bed of crispy noodles

Tempura Sashimi—14.25
with champagne uni sauce

China Grill Exotic Greens—9.50
with miso vinaigrette

Peking Duck Salad—14.50
served crispy with tangerine and orange sauce

Entrees

Grilled Free Range Chicken—19.75
with toasted garlic and small onions

Grilled Marinated Lamb—28.25
with red pepper, roasting peppers
and grilled endive

Grilled Scallops—21.75
with red pepper basil sauce

Sizzling Whole Fish—market
ginger stuffed with ponzu sauce

Shrimp and Noodles—18.75
wok sauteed in spicy uni sauce

Roasted Veal—27.75
in port wine sauce with sauteed mushrooms
in an artichoke cup

Crispy Duck—22.75
honey glazed with plum sauce

Grilled Dry Aged Szechuan Beef—26.75
in hot oil and cilantro

Grilled Special Fish—market
with stir fry asian greens

Shanghai Lobster—market
with ginger, curry and crispy spinach

Grilled Mandarin Beef—25.75
with soy honey orange sauce

Grilled Golden Squab—26.75
on crispy noodles with shiitake plum sauce

Steamed Whole Fish—market
in soy lime sake sauce on a bed of
ribbon vegetables

Rice

Duck Fried Rice—7.75

Five Vegetable Fried Rice—7.25

Vegetable Fried Brown Rice—8.75

VEGETABLES

Wok Sauteed Vegetables—7.00

Crispy Spinach—6.50

Bamboo Steamed Vegetables—8.00

No cigar or pipe smoking, please.

La Bamba Mexican Restaurant & Cantina

ADDRESS: Merced, California, USA

CHEF: Ruben Torres

STYLE OF FOOD: Mexican

NO. OF SEATS: 114

DESIGNER (Interior): Jim Souza

DESIGNER (Graphics): Patricia Belyea/Belyea Design, Seattle, Washington, USA

DATE OF COMPLETION: November 1988

GRAPHIC ELEMENTS: Logo, menu, aprons, polo shirts, T-shirts, table tents, napkins, signage

A nice use of pattern and fresh colours as a secondary device to support and relax the tightly controlled symbol. I also like the use of the little macaw on its own here and there.

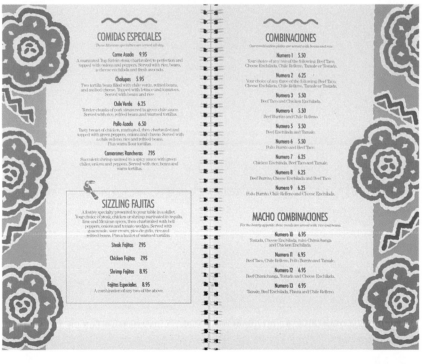

JOIN OUR AMIGO CLUB

Celebrate with us.

Please register so we can say "Thank You" for being our customer.

We will send a card on your birthday or anniversary.

This special card will tell about a free treat waiting for you at La Bamba.

Ask your waitperson for a registration card.

GUAYMAS
COCINA FRESCA REGIONAL ™

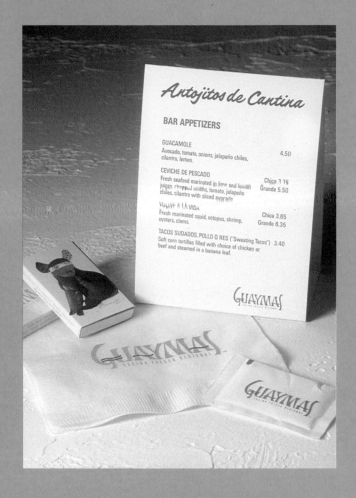

Guaymas

ADDRESS: Tiburon, California, USA

CHEF: Jose Hernandez

STYLE OF FOOD: Mexican cuisine

NO. OF SEATS: 125

DESIGNER (Interior): Ron Nunn & Associates,
Tiburon, California, USA

DESIGNER (Graphics): Elizabeth Berta/
Jody Thompson, The Thompson Design Group,
San Francisco, California, USA

DATE OF COMPLETION: June 1985

GRAPHIC ELEMENTS: Menu, matchbook, beverage
napkins, bar menu, T-shirts, business letterhead
and envelope, business cards

Everything here is secondary to the wonderful
watercolour painting by Nathan Oliveira called
'Scratching Dog', although I can't imagine why it's
appropriate.

REAL COMPAÑIA CERVECERA

CASA FERNANDEZ

1 9 8 8

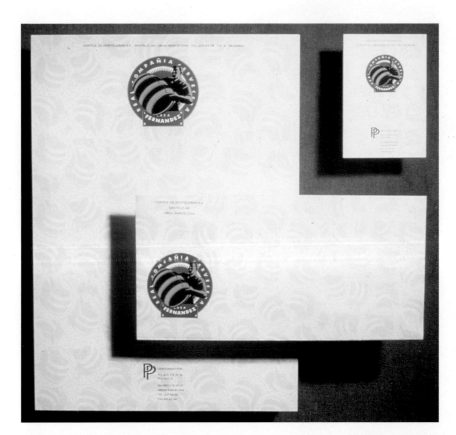

Real Compañia Cervecera Casa Fernandez

ADDRESS: Barcelona, Spain

CHEF: Merce Casanovas

STYLE OF FOOD: Spanish tapas

NO. OF SEATS: 60

DESIGNER (Interior): Carlos Rolando/
CR Communication and Design Services SA,
Barcelona, Spain

DESIGNER (Graphics): Carlos Rolando
CR Communication and Design Services SA,
Barcelona, Spain

DATE OF COMPLETION: May 1989

GRAPHIC ELEMENTS: Logo, door handle,
matchboxes, menu, napkins, business stationery,
table linen, interior mural

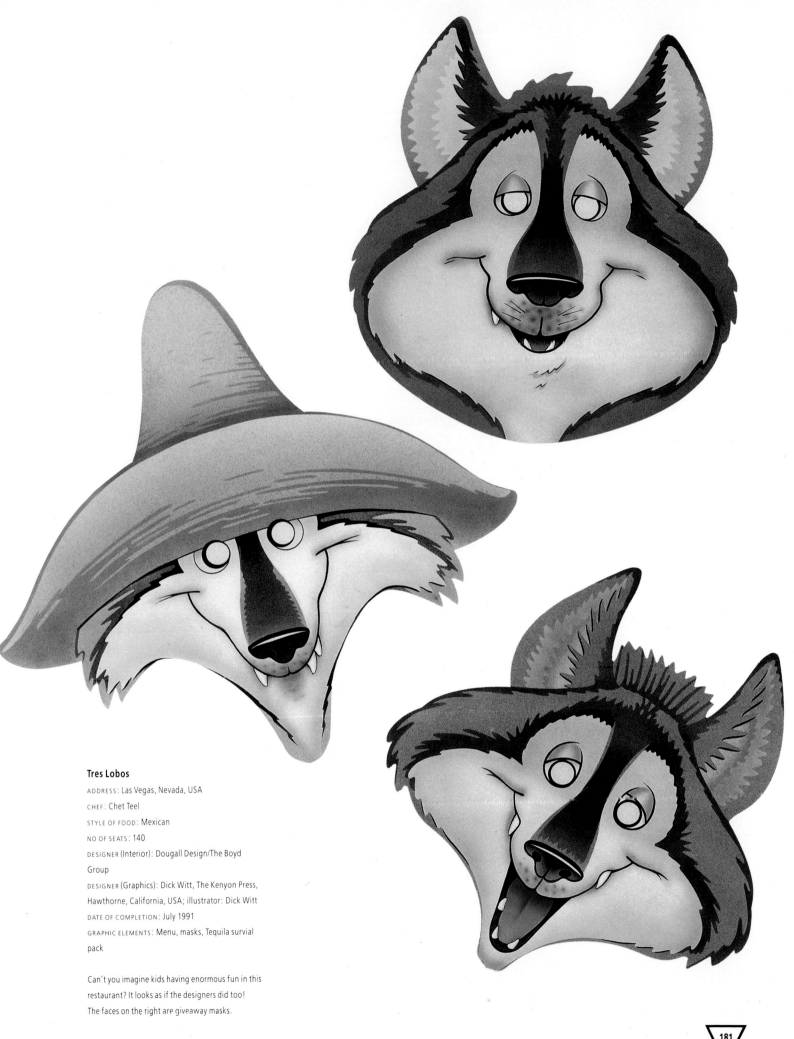

Tres Lobos

ADDRESS: Las Vegas, Nevada, USA

CHEF: Chet Teel

STYLE OF FOOD: Mexican

NO OF SEATS: 140

DESIGNER (Interior): Dougall Design/The Boyd Group

DESIGNER (Graphics): Dick Witt, The Kenyon Press, Hawthorne, California, USA; illustrator: Dick Witt

DATE OF COMPLETION: July 1991

GRAPHIC ELEMENTS: Menu, masks, Tequila survial pack

Can't you imagine kids having enormous fun in this restaurant? It looks as if the designers did too! The faces on the right are giveaway masks.

Ricardos Restaurants

ADDRESS: Nationwide chain throughout the USA

CHEF: Various

STYLE OF FOOD: Mexican family cuisine

NO. OF SEATS: 200 plus bar

DESIGNER (Interior): Dean Gerrie Design,
Santa Ana, California, USA

DESIGNER (Graphics): Dean Gerrie Design,
Santa Ana, California, USA; photography:
Russel Sasaki

DATE OF COMPLETION: 1990

GRAPHIC ELEMENTS: Menu

One of the few menus that use the same typeface
for the logo and menu heading, giving it a useful
carrythrough. The illustration style is well chosen,
to fit with the character of the lettering.

Bar Madrid

ADDRESS: London, England

CHEF: Victor Campos

STYLE OF FOOD: Spanish tapas

NO. OF SEATS: 100

DESIGNER (Interior): Eddie McAtominey, Design House, London, England

DESIGNER (Graphics): Vicky Fullick, Design House, London, England

DATE OF COMPLETION: November 1989

GRAPHIC ELEMENTS: Menus, matchbox, neon signs, window decoration

A nice use of 1950s style typeface and imagery – plus more 'wavy' lines.

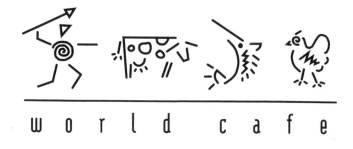

World Cafe

ADDRESS: Santa Monica, California, USA

CHEF: David Tek

STYLE OF FOOD: Eclectic: Jamaican/South American/Californian cuisine

NO. OF SEATS: 60

DESIGNER (Interior): Susan Rogers, Rusty Kay & Associates, Santa Monica, California, USA

DESIGNER (Graphics): Susan Rogers, Rusty Kay & Associates, Santa Monica, California, USA

DATE OF COMPLETION: May 1990

GRAPHIC ELEMENTS: Menu

The owner's idea was to create a restaurant that was both primitive and modern and most of all fun.

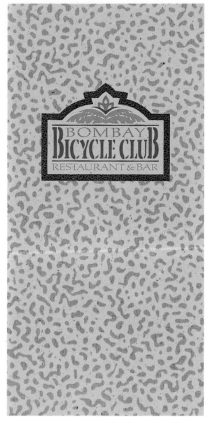

Bombay Bicycle Club

ADDRESS: Nationwide throughout USA

CHEF: Various

STYLE OF FOOD: Theme with tropical accent

NO. OF SEATS: 100 plus bar

DESIGNER (Interior): Dean Gerrie Design,
Santa Ana, California, USA

DESIGNER (Graphics): Dean Gerrie Design,
Santa Ana, California, USA; photography:
Russel Sasaki

DATE OF COMPLETION: 1990

GRAPHIC ELEMENTS: Menu, exterior signage

Catchy name, fun graphics.

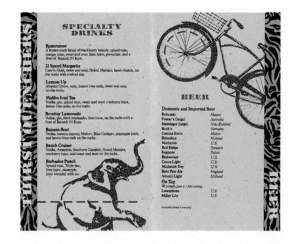

Corporate and Institutional

Restaurants in museums, galleries and shops are no longer the dowdy unloved slaves to necessity they once were. Keen to persuade their customers to stay longer (and spend more), the owners have more radical overhauls. There may not be printed menus but the surroundings are often well planned, comfortable and even trendy with plenty of decorative inspiration drawn from the wealth of material on hand nearby.

Science Museum Café

ADDRESS: London, England

CHEF: De Blank Restaurants

STYLE OF FOOD: Café chic

NO. OF SEATS: 100

DESIGNER (Interior): Peter Leonard Associates, London, England

DESIGNER (Graphics): Peter Leonard Associates, London, England

DATE OF COMPLETION: November-1990

GRAPHIC ELEMENTS: Logo and signage

Sitting as it does at one end of the airplane collection, this cafe draws inspiration from its surroundings. Even the choice of chairs reflect aircraft technology.

Next Café

ADDRESS: Nationwide UK

CHEF: Numerous

STYLE OF FOOD: Pâtisserie and café style

NO. OF SEATS: From 25 to 100

DESIGNER (Interior): David Davies Associates, London, England

DESIGNER (Graphics): David Davies Associates, London, England

DATE OF COMPLETION: 1987

GRAPHIC ELEMENTS: Signage, menus, wine bottles

Beautifully subtle graphic branding, this is one of a series of in-store cafes and coffee shops.

St ANNS

St Ann's Court

ADDRESS: London, England

STYLE OF FOOD: From a nut to a Pizza bar

NO. OF SEATS: 250 (approximately)

DESIGNER (Interior): David Davies Associates,
London, England

DESIGNER (Graphics): David Davies Associates,
London, England

DATE OF COMPLETION: 1989

GRAPHIC ELEMENTS: Restaurant signage, menus

The graphics have been carefully worked into the
interior concept rather than applied afterwards.

The Review Restaurant

ADDRESS: Royal Festival Hall, London, England

CHEF: Peter O'Sullivan

STYLE OF FOOD: Modern light international cuisine

NO. OF SEATS: 100 (350 for parties)

DESIGNER (Interior): RSCG Conran Design, London, England

DESIGNER (Graphics): David Birt, RSCG Conran Design, London, England

DATE OF COMPLETION: May 1988

GRAPHIC ELEMENTS: Menus, plates, napkins, signage

The inspiration here comes from the undulating ceiling panel and the venue's situation overlooking the Thames.

London's restaurant by the river

British Airways Staff Canteen

ADDRESS: Gatwick Airport, Crawley, Surrey, England

CHEF: Sutcliffe Catering

STYLE OF FOOD: Self Service

NO. OF SEATS: 145

DESIGNER (Interior): Tilney Lumsden Shane Ltd, London, England

DESIGNER (Graphics): Tilney Lumsden Shane Ltd, London, England

DATE OF COMPLETION: February 1991

GRAPHIC ELEMENTS: Glass screens, menu board

Graphics seem to involve every aspect of this crisp, clean staff canteen. Only the menu is kept simple and undecorated.

The Café in the Zoo

ADDRESS: London Zoo, London, England

CHEF: Various

STYLE OF FOOD: Family

NO. OF SEATS: 100

DESIGNER (Interior): Minale Tattersfield, London, England

DESIGNER (Graphics): Brian Tatterfield, Minale Tattersfield, London, England

DATE OF COMPLETION: 1984

GRAPHIC ELEMENTS: Signage, menus, plates, clocks, napkins, sachets

A nice conjunction of witty typography and simple cut-out signs.

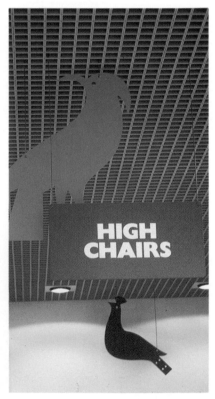

Slices Plus

ADDRESS: Various; part of the Seiler Corporation a
food service organisation catering for corporate,
hospital, college and university cafeterias. The
Seiler Corporation headquarters is at 153 Second
Avenue, Waltham, Massachusetts 02254, USA

CHEF: Various

STYLE OF FOOD: Pizzas, sandwiches, snacks

NO. OF SEATS: Varies with location

DESIGNER (Interior): Varies with location

DESIGNER (Graphics): Cindy Guernsey and Luis
Camano, Donya Melanson Associates, Boston,
Massachusetts, USA; poster illustration by Bruce
Sanders; backpack illustration by Bob Cline

DATE OF COMPLETION: January 1990

GRAPHIC ELEMENTS: Poster, POP backpack
counter card display to hold pizza box menus
(customized for individual institutions), button/
badge, Slices Plus signage

While it does not look exactly 'tasty', I like the
simple graphic illustration that ends with CRUMBS.

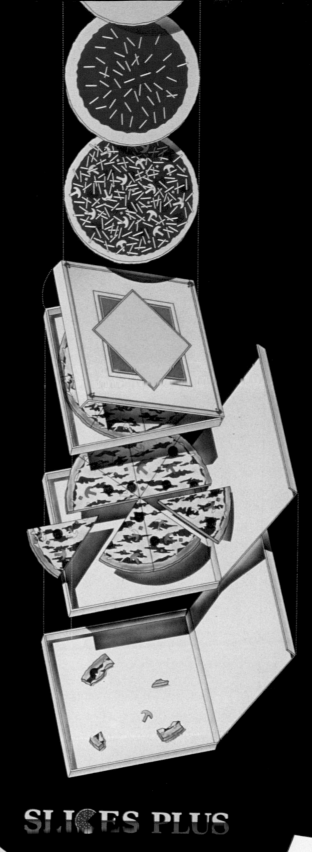

SLICES PLUS

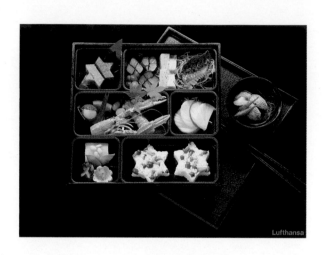

Lufthansa

Food in Transit

The dining rooms in the grand old ocean liners of the 1920s and 1930s had beautifully designed and printed menus that often illustrated their ports of call. More recently, airlines have been much more subtle and imaginative in their solutions and now with increasing competition for passengers, even railways are starting to catch up.

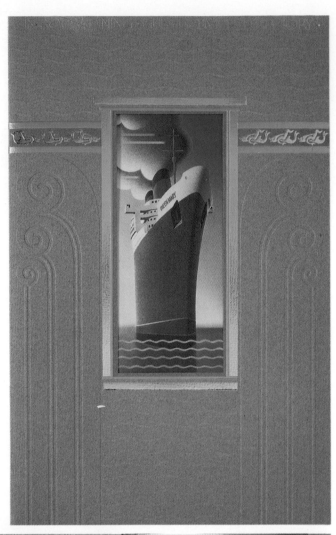

Queen Mary Hotel

ADDRESS: Long Beach, California, USA

CHEF: Brad Toles

STYLE OF FOOD: Room Service

NO OF SEATS: 365 state rooms

DESIGNER (Graphics): Dick Witt, The Kenyon Press,
Hawthorne, California, USA; illustrator:
Robert Greisen

DATE OF COMPLETION: January 1990

GRAPHIC ELEMENTS: Dining/Guest Services
Directory, menu

By a successful use of colour and texture, this
solution conjures up some of the elegance of travel
on a luxury liner.

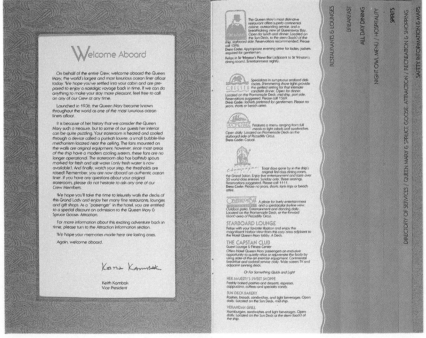

LONDON · NEW YORK
3h50

THE CONCORDE MENU

LONDON · NEW YORK
BA 001 CON B3 25—04

LONDON · NEW YORK

MORNING MEAL

APPETIZERS
Canapé selection including smoked beef with
asparagus, caviar and smoked salmon

Refreshing combination of chilled mango and
fresh fruits in season

MAIN COURSES

Fillet of beef, lamb and pork, seared on a
hot griddle and flavoured with a savoury gravy
Served with leaf spinach, tomato and crisp pitta
case of maître d'hôtel potatoes

or

The Concorde brunch featuring fluffy
scrambled eggs enveloped in a wafer thin slice
of smoked Scottish salmon
Garnished with mushrooms, tomato
and spears of fresh asparagus

LONDON · NEW YORK

LONDON · NEW YORK

or

As a light alternative may we suggest our
cold collation featuring honey glazed breast of
corn-fed chicken and country style ham

SALAD BOWL
Mixed seasonal salad
Served with vinaigrette dressing

DESSERT
Variety of fresh fruit and berries set in
a light Champagne gelée

ASSORTED CHEESE
A selection of English Stilton,
Farmhouse Cheshire and French Comté cheese
with butter, crackers and crudités

COFFEE – TEA
Coffee, decaffeinated coffee or tea
Served with a selection of friandises

LONDON · NEW YORK

Concorde

CHEF: Anton Mosimann

STYLE OF FOOD: International cuisine

NO. OF SEATS: 100

DESIGNER (Graphics): British Airways Design,
London, England

DATE OF COMPLETION: 1990

GRAPHIC ELEMENTS: Menus, napkins, china

Nicely understated use of elegant typography and
white space, something that designers often forget
about. There is something ironical about a menu
twice the size of the windows on board Concorde,
in which space is so cramped.

THE CONCORDE CELLAR
· ONE ·

CHAMPAGNE
MOËT & CHANDON
CUVÉE DOM PÉRIGNON 1980
Dom Pérignon, named after the celebrated
Benedictine Abbey treasurer who (in
legend, not fact) "invented" Champagne,
was the original Champagne "cuvée de
luxe" and remains unsurpassed in finesse,
subtlety and authority of style. The 1980
vintage is now showing the signs of
maturity: full straw colour, bouquet
suggesting sweet biscuits, silky texture and
creamy taste. Young, this wine was almost
ethereal; mature it is supremely graceful.

Michael Broadbent
Michael Broadbent MW

Hugh Johnson
Hugh Johnson

THE CONCORDE CELLAR
· THIRTEEN ·

CHÂTEAU TALBOT 1978
GRAND CRU CLASSÉ,
SAINT-JULIEN
Talbot is an immaculately run estate and its
wine is consistent in style, allowing for the
vagaries of the weather in Bordeaux. 1978,
known as the year of the miracle, was nearly a
disaster. A poor spring and dismal summer
were saved by perfect weather during ripening
and throughout the harvest. The wine is still
deep in colour though showing its maturity; a
rich, ripe and spicy bouquet, with the
blackcurrant character of Cabernet Sauvignon;
a touch of sweetness on the palate, nice weight
and good fruit.
A well-developed and attractive claret.

Michael Broadbent
Michael Broadbent MW

Hugh Johnson
Hugh Johnson

Lufthansa
Business Class
Menu

Lufthansa
Business Class
Menu

Lufthansa

ADDRESS: Worldwide; national carrier of Germany

CHEF: Various

STYLE OF FOOD: International

NO. OF SEATS: Depends on aircraft
configuration

DESIGNER (Graphics): First Class menus: Klaus
Willie, Lufthansa Design, Cologne, Germany;
photography by Wolfgang Arnhold, Frankfurt,
Germany; Business Class menus: Klaus Willie,
Lufthansa Design, Cologne, Germany;
photography by Siegfried Himmer, Cologne,
Germany

GRAPHIC ELEMENTS: Menus

No hint of a frozen, pre-cooked or pre-packed
about these graphics. The photography is as fresh
as the produce; at the same time it avoids the 'art
photography' syndrome and doesn't include
unrealistic ingredients.

Lufthansa
Business Class
Menu

Lufthansa
Business Class
Menu

Lufthansa
Business Class
Menu

Lufthansa
Business Class
Menu

Lufthansa continued over page

Lufthansa continued

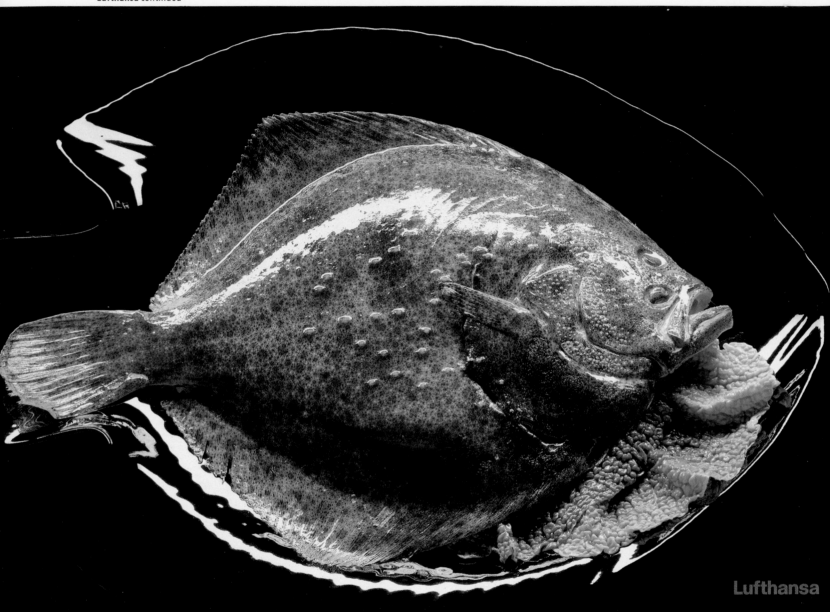

Lufthansa

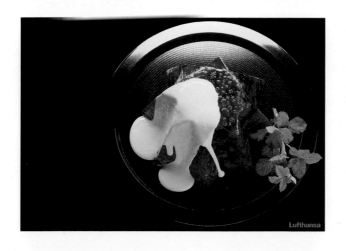

BA First Class

ADDRESS: Worldwide on BA flights

STYLE OF FOOD: Exquisite traditional

NO. OF SEATS: 18

DESIGNER (Interior): David Davies Associates,
London, England

DESIGNER (Graphics): David Davies Associates,
London, England

DATE OF COMPLETION: 1989

GRAPHIC ELEMENTS: Menus, plates, napkins,
tablecloths, glasses

A strong resemblance here to college blazers and
Old School Ties.

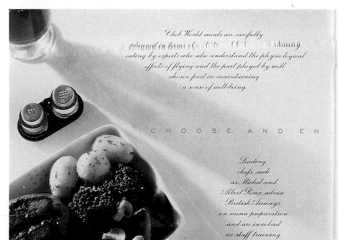

Club World meals are carefully planned to encourage healthy eating by experts who also understand the physiological effects of flying and the part played by well chosen food in maintaining a sense of well-being.

Leading chefs, such as Michel and Albert Roux, advise British Airways on menu preparation and are involved in staff training programmes.

CHOOSE AND ENJOY YOUR FAVOURITE FOOD

Great care has been taken in the preparation of Club World menus to ensure that passengers enjoy the best of fare, food that's full of natural flavour, prepared to immaculate standards.

In the main meal, the full Club World tray carries a superb hors d'oeuvres, which is replaced later by the passenger's choice of entrée. Of three main courses, one is normally a gourmet-style dish, one a grill or similar plain alternative and the third an attractive lighter cold collation.

On most flights, the full tray is then replaced by a half tray bearing a delicious dessert, coffee cup and chocolates. There's then service of cheeses and port followed later by liqueurs.

All Club World menus reflect the trend towards

BA Club Class

ADDRESS: British Airways, London, England

STYLE OF FOOD: Traditional

NO. OF SEATS: 100

DESIGNER (Interior): David Davies Associates,
London, England

DESIGNER (Graphics): David Davies Associates,
London, England

DATE OF COMPLETION: 1989

GRAPHIC ELEMENTS: Menu, plates, glasses, cruet
sets, salt and pepper pots, trays, matchboxes,
napkins

One of the most successful transformation jobs in
recent years, this simple graphic concept has been
meticulously translated onto hundreds of in-flight
items, from toothpaste to glasses, and has elevated
club class travel from a clever marketing idea to a
desirable status symbol.

CLUB ^(SM)

WORLD

BRITISH AIRWAYS

BA Club Class continued over page

BA Club Class continued

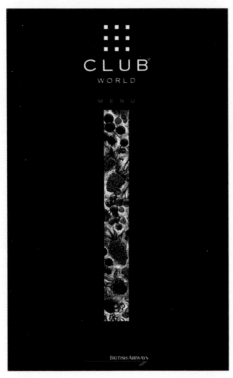

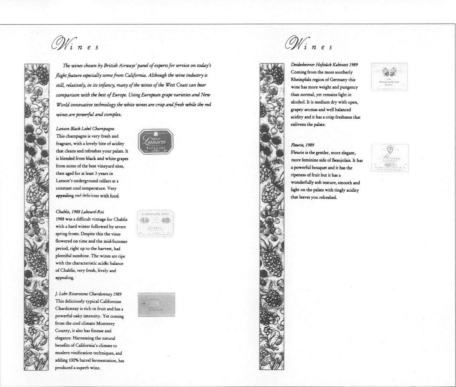

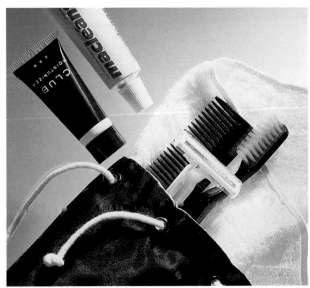

Swissair

ADDRESS: Zürich, Switzerland

CHEF: Catering chief: G. Lorenz

STYLE OF FOOD: International

NO OF SEATS: Varies with aircraft configuration

DESIGNER (Graphics): Sabine Schroer (illustrator)

DATE OF COMPLETION: 1989

GRAPHIC ELEMENTS: Menus

swissair

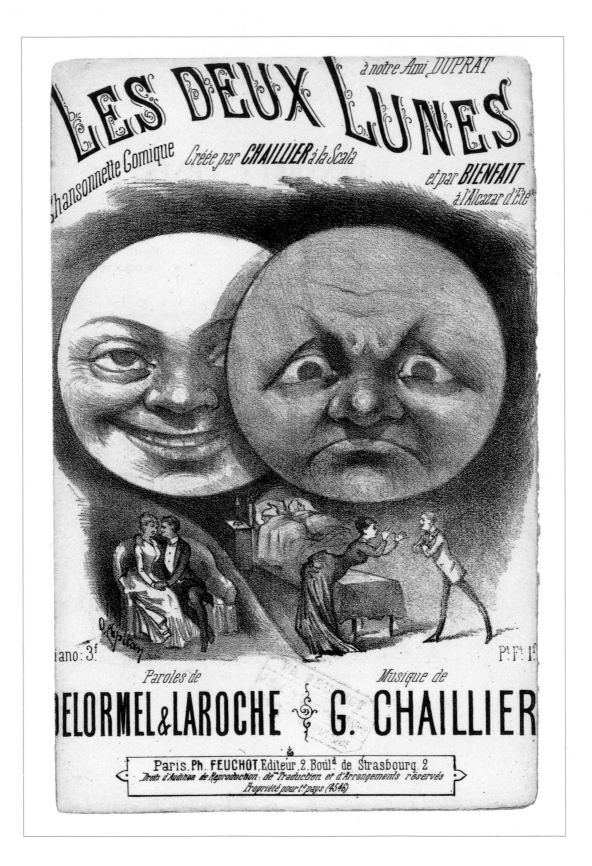

Air France

ADDRESS: Paris, France

CHEF: Various

STYLE OF FOOD: French/International

NO. OF SEATS: Varies

DESIGNER (Graphics): Air France Design, Paris, France

DATE OF COMPLETION: 1990

GRAPHIC ELEMENTS: Menu

A wonderfully original solution. Each menu comes in a variety of facsimile piano music covers, an idea that is both witty and totally French.

Intercity

ADDRESS: c/o British Rail Intercity, London, England

CHEF: David Small

STYLE OF FOOD: International

NO. OF SEATS: Varies

DESIGNER (Graphics): Newell and Sorrell Ltd, London, England

DATE OF COMPLETION: 1987 and ongoing

GRAPHIC ELEMENTS: Menu, stationery

This solution elevates the train to the status of airline travel – and why not?

Wagon Lits

ADDRESS: Restaurant Ferroviaire du T.G.V., SNCF, France

CHEF: Various

STYLE OF FOOD: French

NO. OF SEATS: Varies depending on rolling stock

DESIGNER (Graphics): Christiana Sofianofoulou/ Style Marque, Paris, France

DATE OF COMPLETION: 1988

GRAPHIC ELEMENTS: Menu, napkins, dishes

By combining strong corporate branding with clean graphics, this designer creates an effective solution without promising something the client can't deliver.

Venice Simplon Orient Express Pullman

ADDRESS: London, England

CHEF: Leith's Good Food, London, England

SYTLE OF FOOD: Silver Service Country House style

NUMBER OF SEATS: 20, 24 or 26 (depending on carriage)

DESIGNER (Interior): Gerard Gallet

DATE OF COMPLETION: 1982

GRAPHIC ELEMENTS: All china, menu, cutlery, napkins, tablecloths, glassware, vases, table lamps, ashtrays, matches

This solution succeeds because of its simplicity and understatement; with all the rich imagery available, it would have been easy to go too far.

Index of Projects